COMMERCIALIZATION
OF SPACE

L. B. TAYLOR, JR.

COMMERCIALIZATION OF SPACE

Fairfax Baptist Temple
9524 Braddock Road
Fairfax, Virginia 22032

Franklin Watts
New York/London/Toronto/Sydney/1987
An Impact Book

Photographs courtesy of:
NASA: pp. 20, 54, 57,
60, 73, 96, 106, 107, 117;
COMSAT Corporation: pp. 42, 45;
Rockwell International: p. 76;
National Bureau of Standards: p. 87.

Library of Congress Cataloging-in-Publication Data

Taylor, L. B.
Commercialization of space.

(An Impact book)
Includes index.
Summary: Discusses plans, opportunities, and
possibilities for the commercialization of space by
private industry in such areas as tourism, research,
mining, surveillance, communication, and spinoffs
from space technology.
1. Space industrialization—United States—Juvenile
literature. [1. Space industrialization] I. Title.
HD9711.75.U62T39 1987 338.0919 86–9224
ISBN 0–531–10236–X

*This book is for
Ann Black.*

CONTENTS

COMMERCIALIZATION
O F S P A C E

CHAPTER ONE

THE BUSINESS OF SPACE

Text and history books note that the space age officially began with the Soviet Union's launch of *Sputnik 1*, a tiny satellite, on October 4, 1957, and that on July 20, 1969, the United States became the first country to put a human on the moon.

Yet two other dates several years later may eventually prove to be the most significant of all, at least in regard to long-term benefits of space for mankind. On April 12, 1981, the initial test flight of the United States space shuttle was successfully achieved. And on July 4, 1982, in a major address, President Ronald Reagan set a new national space policy, asking NASA (the National Aeronautics and Space Administration) to begin effecting a transition that would lead to the operational use of space programs and systems by the nation's private businesses.

Thus, the events that took place on these latter two dates unofficially launched the era of the commercialization of space, proving what had long been envisioned—that the day would come when not only earth orbit, but the infinite reaches beyond it would be opened up to practical commerce. The dawning of that day has arrived.

Already, we are reaping benefits from this technological bonanza all around us, often without even realizing it. We take for granted, for example, the instantaneous televising of world events without even thinking that they are being made possible only through the relaying of signals to batteries of communications satellites positioned more than 22,000 miles (35,000 km) above the earth.

We routinely view daily photographs, taken from space, which give us the most accurate weather forecasts in history, and provide us with ample warning of approaching storms. Thousands of images sent to earth every day from remote-sensing satellites in earth orbit provide geologists, hydrologists, forest experts, farmers, cartographers, oceanographers, and hosts of other specialists with enormous amounts of valuable information, which helps them better manage the world's precious resources.

Navigation satellites, feeding position data to shipboard computers, enable vessels to sail on perfect, prescribed courses. Military surveillance spacecraft keep unblinking electronic eyes on troop, armor, aircraft, and missile placements and movements all over the world, transmitting the data instantaneously to intelligence centers for analysis and tracking. From orbital vantage points, sensitive instruments aboard satellites detect and pinpoint environmental polluters and relay the information back to land stations.

More down-to-earth are the thousands of space technology "spinoff" benefits that are improving our way of life. Through the efforts of NASA and of imaginative entrepreneurs, thousands of spinoffs have been generated over the last twenty-five years, spanning a broad range of public needs and conveniences. Such technology has been successfully transferred to the fields of medicine, public safety, transportation, industrial processes, pollution control, energy systems, construction, law enforcement, home apliances, farm machinery, sports and recreation, food products, and to other areas.

Examples include everything from new, improved, and miniaturized heart pacemakers to nonflammable foams, paints, and fabrics . . . from search and rescue beacons to solar heating units and solar cell arrays for efficient energy . . . from freeze-dried foods (first developed for astronauts on space flights) to heat-resistant coatings in cookwear . . . and from digital clocks to long-lasting batteries.

Benefits from past and present space efforts already have worked their way into our daily lives—to a far greater extent than most of us realize. Impressive as these contributions have been, however, they represent only the tip of a gigantic iceberg of future values that are just now beginning to be realized and understood.

The development of the space shuttle reusable orbital transportation system in the 1980s, and the presidential mandate to construct a permanent station in earth orbit in the 1990s, are opening the space frontier to the age of commercialization. And the magnitudes this era will reach in the years to come cannot even be conceived at this date. Who, for example, in December 1903, when the Wright brothers first flew their flimsy aircraft at Kitty Hawk, North Carolina, could have envisioned the world's multi-billion-dollar airline industry today? Who could have foreseen how it has dramatically changed our lives?

Yet, in time, space commercialization will dwarf the airline industry. The Center for Space Policy, an organization formed in 1983 to evaluate commercial opportunities in space, estimates a market of $44 billion to $53 billion by the year 2000. Some experts feel even that may be conservative. In his introductory remarks for a special NASA publication, *Space Spinoff 1984*, former NASA administrator James Beggs estimated that the market will be "several hundred billion dollars." And U.S. Congressmen Newt Gingrich of Georgia and Bob Walker of Pennsylvania think it is possible to create, by the year 2000, a half-trillion-dollar space-based world economy, one that could generate twenty million jobs on the earth.

Peering further into the future, L. W. Lehr, an executive with the 3M Company (Minnesota Mining and Manufacturing), which already has committed millions of dollars to space research, predicts a market that could reach anywhere from $75 billion to $3.5 trillion by the year 2050.

Breaking out some of these projections, the Center for Space Policy forecasts, by 2000, up to $20 billion in gross annual revenues for the production of pharmaceuticals in space; $5 billion for materials processing in space; $15 billion to $20 billion in commercial communications; $1 billion to $2 billion in the servicing of satellites; and $1 billion in commercial launch operations.

Already today the space communications industry does more than $3-billion worth of business annually, and employs, directly or indirectly, more than one million people, mostly Americans.

Said former NASA administrator Beggs: "The development of space-relayed communications was the first effort to commercialize space and it is so far the most economically successful. In coming years, however, we can expect to see much broader pursuit of business space opportunities. Essentially there are three areas of commercial space promise. One is the operation of satellites for communications, or for a variety of other practical applications involving observation of the earth from orbit. A second is provision of services to satellite operators—building space systems, launching them, or processing and analyzing the data they supply. The third—and perhaps the most exciting —is manufacture in orbit of products that cannot be made on the earth, products that promise societal and economic benefits of immense order.

"President Reagan's initiative to build a permanently manned orbital station significantly advances the prospects for space commercialization," Beggs said. "It is a plan that builds upon the highly successful policies of earlier years, when the nation expanded and strengthened its economy through publicly funded development of highways, railroads, and airports. . . . The space station program will assure the United States industrial community that the government will create the foundation essential to private sector investment in space. It will enable government and industry to forge a new partnership toward realizing the commercial potential of the space realm.

"As we embark on the second quarter-century of American space endeavor, we stand on the threshold of an exciting new era. The space station and the complementary space transportation system [shuttle] will enormously broaden our national capability for exploiting space and open new avenues of opportunity for benefit to mankind—not only commercial benefits, but the equally important, if less visible, benefits that will accrue from advanced scientific research in space. To quote the president's summation: 'We can follow our dreams to distant stars, living and working in space for peaceful, economic, and scientific gain.' "

CHAPTER TWO

FROM EXPLORATION TO EXPLOITATION

In the 1960s, NASA's overriding objective—as dictated in May 1961 by President John F. Kennedy—was to make a successful manned lunar landing before the end of the decade. While the space agency continued to launch satellites into earth orbit, and occasionally sent unmanned spacecraft on long-distance flights to neighboring planets in the solar system, the major effort was centered on the moon mission. That was culminated in spectacular fashion in July 1969 when astronauts Neil Armstrong and Buzz Aldrin planted the flag of the United States on lunar terrain. It was a magnificent engineering, scientific, technological, and human feat—perhaps the greatest in the history of mankind—that was applauded all over the world.

Several other flights to the moon were made. But in the 1970s, public interest started to wane. People began to ask such questions as, "So we've landed men on the moon and machines on Mars, so what? What good does it do me on the earth?" Pressured to come up with the answers, NASA began to redirect the thrust of its programs.

"We are turning from a period of space exploration to one of space exploitation," said NASA administrator James C. Fletcher at the time. "We have come up with a balanced space plan for the seventies. We are increasing our capability to do useful work in all the major areas of space activity.

"We have entered a period of increasing earthly benefits from the space program," Fletcher said. "We will, of course, continue to look outward at the universe, but we are devoting increased attention to the study of our own home planet from the vantage point of space. We can now turn our hard-won new abilities to increasingly practical use. The space program is giving us the tools to help solve many of earth's most pressing problems."

Elaborating on this, Dale D. Myers, former NASA associate administrator for manned space flight, said: "We have moved from the era of learning how to live and work in space to a new plateau, where this nation can utilize space and its unique capabilities for expanding its horizons in science and in applications, in defense, commercial activities, and in international cooperation, at reduced costs. The challenge facing us now is to consolidate, to redefine and to apply what we learned as we move into the era of space utilization for man's benefit."

One of the keys to this transition from exploration to exploitation, NASA felt, would be the development of a reliable, reusable space transportation system, to be called the space shuttle. On January 5, 1972, President Richard M. Nixon declared: "The United States should proceed at once with the development of an entirely new type of space transportation system designed to help transform the space frontier of the 1970s into familiar territory, easily accessible for human endeavor in the 1980s and 1990s.

"This system will center on a space vehicle that can shuttle repeatedly from earth to orbit and back . . . it will go a long way toward delivering the rich benefits of practical space use and the valuable spinoffs from space efforts into the daily lives of Americans and all people."

But before the billions of dollars the shuttle's development would cost could be committed, it had to be established that humans could safely live and work in space for extended periods of time. Prior to this time, most of the manned flights had lasted only a few hours or days. With the shuttle flights calling for periods of orbit ranging from a week to a month or longer, more data on the long-term effects of space on humans had to be obtained. Hundreds of complex questions had to be answered.

Such answers came through a program in the early 1970s called Skylab. Its concept was simple. NASA would launch into orbit a refurbished third stage of the *Saturn 5* moon rocket—a huge cylindrical shell 48 feet (15 m) long and 21 feet (6 m) in diameter, encompassing about 10,000 cubic feet (280 cu m) of space.

In effect, this stage would serve as a temporary space station in earth orbit. It was designed to include both living and laboratory working areas in a two-story arrangement. Teams of astronauts then would be flown to and from Skylab. And throughout 1973 and into 1974, three 3-man crews did just that, conducting a great number of experiments and tests to advance people's capabilities to live and work in the space environment.

As just one example, the astronauts trained banks of highly sensitive instruments on strips of land and sea 270 miles (435 km) below to document surface features. The resulting data was used for mapping and studying geographic areas and geologic structures; for determining weather characteristics and patterns; for sighting crop and forestry cover; and for determining the health of vegetation, the types and conditions of soil, water storage, sea surface temperatures, and wind and sea conditions.

Possibly most important of all, Skylab proved that humans could thrive and function well in the zero-gravity environment of earth orbit. This was exactly the type of information needed to go ahead confidently with development of the shuttle.

Skylab in Earth orbit in 1974. Here astronauts conducted experiments related to people living and working in a space environment.

What emerged, after years of study and design, was a versatile vehicle that could be launched into space by conventional, strap-on rockets, maneuver in orbit much like a spacecraft, and then fly back to earth and land like an airplane. The shuttle is an engineering marvel. The orbiter itself looks like a snub-nosed, fat airliner. It is 122 feet (37 m) long with a wingspan of only 78 feet (24 m). Its vast cargo bay measures 60 feet (18 m) in length and can carry payloads up to 65,000 pounds (29,484 kg) into orbit.

The three-story cabin is designed as a combination working and living area that can accommodate several people. The upper section contains the flight deck and is much like that of a jetliner. The midsection includes passenger seating, the living area, with working, sleeping, dining, and bathroom facilities, and compartments for electronic equipment. The living area is roughly equivalent in size to one-fourth the area of a small three-bedroom house.

Following years of preparation and exhaustive testing, the first shuttle, *Columbia*, was successfully flown into orbit April 12, 1981, launching the new era of space transportation. Over the next few years, flights became almost routine as the shuttle passed from test flight to operational status.

With the transition from exploration to exploitation under way, the time had come for NASA to begin the process of turning over the business of space development to private industry.

CHAPTER THREE

TURNING OVER
THE REINS

There is a historic precedent for the space commercialization movement. The transfer of major responsibilities from government to private industry happened earlier this century with the aviation industry. But this did not happen until the government had overseen the formative years of the young industry. Had it not been for government support early in the twentieth century, flying machines might have been grounded for years or even decades before it became practical for businesses to make large developmental investments in such a risky venture.

The government was initially interested in the military potential of aircraft, and set up a system of aeronautical research laboratories to encourage the new technology. As the practical applications of this fledgling industry became apparent, private corporations began to get involved, first by building aircraft, and later by operating them commercially. But even as these companies entered the industry, the government fostered growth through the purchase of military aircraft and the granting of contracts for airmail delivery. In time, the aviation industry became less and less dependent on federal backing. It appears the space industry is following this pattern.

And there already is a precedent here. NASA has accumulated a long and proud history of working closely and productively with private enterprises. NASA space programs have been based on participation and contribution by three segments of our society—government, industry, and academic institutions.

Since its earliest days, NASA has employed industries and universities as contractors. Since 1962, NASA has provided launch services for privately owned commercial communications satellites. Beginning in 1972, NASA has entered into "partnership" arrangements with private firms for the commercial use of space. Now, the nature and character of NASA's relationship with private enterprise is changing still more. To persuade private investors to become involved in new space endeavors, NASA must be responsive to the needs and wants of these investors.

To help facilitate a smooth transition from government to private industry, a National Commercial Space Policy was established late in 1984, along with a congressional amendment to the NASA Space Act of 1958. These direct NASA to "seek and encourage, to the maximum extent possible, the fullest commercial use of space," said James Beggs, former NASA administrator.

To forge the new space policy, NASA formed a special task force in mid-1983. In presenting its findings, the task force said, "The new chapter in the U.S. space program that opened early in this decade with the first flights of the shuttle is now reaching a new phase: space technology is ripe for its transition from exploration to major exploitation, from experimentation to expanded profitable commercial uses." The task force reached the following conclusions:

Commercial activities in space by private enterprise should be expanded now if our nation is to retain and improve its leadership in science and technology, its high living standards, and its advantage in international trade.

With firm resolve and the commitment of reasonable resources over a number of years, government and private enterprise, working together, can turn space into a realm of immense benefit for our nation.

A positive National Commercial Space Policy should be implemented to expedite the expansion of self-sustaining, profit-earning, tax-paying, jobs-providing commercial space activities.

The policy is designed to help reduce the risks of doing business in space. To cut down on technical risks, NASA will conduct and stimulate additional research relevant to commercial developments in space. To reduce financial risks, NASA will provide easy and inexpensive access to orbit as well as to experimental ground facilities.

The policy also calls for the government to reach out and establish new links with the private sector "to stimulate the development of private businesses in space." To effect this, NASA is expanding its traditional links with the aerospace industry and academia to also embrace other industries, such as new high-technology entrepreneurial ventures, and the financial and nonaerospace industrial and academic communities.

NASA also is expanding and targeting the flow of scientific information to spur domestic space commerce projects. And the agency is using public announcements, interviews, speeches, press releases, and articles in technical and business journals to provide information about commercialization opportunities to industry, academia, and the American public.

Implementation of the National Commercial Space Policy is to be guided by these five principles:

1. The government should reach out to establish new links with the private sector, as mentioned previously.

2. Regardless of the government's view of a project's feasibility, it should not impede private efforts to undertake commercial space ventures. If the private sector is willing to make the necessary investment, the project's feasibility should be allowed to be determined by the marketplace and the creativity of the entrepreneur rather than the government's opinion of its viability.

3. If the private sector can operate a space venture more efficiently than the government, then such commercialization should be encouraged. When developing new public space programs, the government should actively consider the view of, and the potential effect on, private ventures.

4. The government should invest in financially promising research and space facilities that encourage private investment. However, the government should not expend tax dollars for endeavors the private sector is willing to underwrite. This will provide at least two benefits. First, it will enable NASA to concentrate a greater percentage of its resources on advancing the technological state of the art in areas where the investment is too great for the private sector. Second, it will engage the private sector's applications and marketing skills for getting space benefits to the people.

5. When a substantial government contribution to a commercial endeavor is requested, two requirements must be met. First, the private sector must have significant capital to risk, and second, there must be significant potential benefits for the nation.

To get the ball rolling, NASA, in 1985, began to help the private sector establish new "centers for commercial development" around the nation. Each center will receive up to $750,000 per year from NASA for three years, plus funds from businesses to support ground or space research important to commercial space ventures. Basic research into programs that could be helped by space processing will be a key function of these centers, forming the groundwork necessary for later orbital testing, research, and development.

In addition, much of NASA's annual budget for "technology utilization," which ran to $11 million in 1985, is being oriented toward commercial space applications. This does not include the $30 million budgeted under NASA's commercial programs office. NASA also has said it will direct more of its own research to commercial space needs, such as orbital materials processing.

Commenting on the policy before the House Subcommittee on Space Technology, former NASA administrator Beggs said: "Space commercialization can have profound impact on the future of our nation. We already know from our experiences with highly profitable, privately owned communications satellites that free enterprise in space can work well. New leaps in technology which are likely to emerge from private initiatives in space could have major implications for the national economy, individual living standards and life-styles, industrial activities, and jobs and international trade.

"The rewards can be immense for our nation."

CHAPTER FOUR

COMMUTER LAUNCH TO SPACE

The first rocket launchings in the United States were carried out by German engineers and scientists. In those days—the mid to late 1940s—the United States had virtually no national expertise of its own, which is somewhat ironic in that an American, Dr. Robert Goddard, is considered one of the pioneers of rocketry. His experiments and testing in the 1920s and 1930s were mostly ignored by his fellow countrymen.

But during the latter part of World War II, the Germans clearly demonstrated both the awesome destructive power of rockets used as weapons, and their long-term potential as space boosters. As World War II ended, there was a mad scramble by the Soviet Union and the United States to collect and import the German experts. The American team was headed by Dr. Wernher von Braun, a brilliant space visionist.

Von Braun and his staff worked for the U.S. Army. In fact, from the mid-1940s to the late 1950s, all rocket or missile launches were for military purposes, and there was a lot of rivalry among the Army, Navy, and Air Force. It was this rivalry, plus a good bit of government bureaucratic bungling, incidentally, that enabled the Russians to beat America into space, on October 4, 1957, when they launched a tiny satellite, *Sputnik 1*, into earth orbit.

Von Braun and the Army had been ready to launch a U.S. satellite for some time, but their proven Redstone-Jupiter rocket was shelved, so the Navy could make an orbital attempt with a Vanguard rocket. Only after the Vanguard program was delayed for months, the Soviets orbited *Sputnik*, and finally, a Vanguard rocket blew up on its launch pad at Cape Canaveral, did Von Braun get an okay to launch his Redstone-Jupiter rocket. Less than four months later, on January 31, 1958, his team successfully orbited the first American spacecraft, *Explorer 1*.

It was not until after NASA was formed, in 1958, that the United States began launching rockets into space for peaceful purposes. And most of these flights through the years have been made on rocket systems initially designed as intermediate and intercontinental ballistic missiles for the armed services, such as the Army's Redstone, and the Air Force's Thor, Atlas, and Titan.

All of these rockets are known as expendable launch vehicles, or ELVs. That is, they were designed for one use only. Once the booster rocket's engines fired their payload into space, the rocket itself fell back to the earth and sank into the Atlantic Ocean. This was, and still is, a very expensive means of transportation.

This cost is one of the primary reasons NASA developed the space shuttle—a reusable system that can be flown to and from space many times. But as versatile and capable as the shuttle is, there is no way it can handle all of the rapidly increasing demands for launching payloads into space.

These demands involve especially the growing requirements of the private sector, such as with commercial communications satellites. There is, and will continue to be, a large demand for conventional expendable-rocket launches. While it is in a way wasteful that the boosters and engines from these launches cannot be recovered for reuse, the ELV launches are, nevertheless, still considerably less expensive than a shuttle flight, which averages $75 million.

As the evolution from government-sponsored space exploration and experimentation to commercialization continued, NASA began to put together the framework of a plan that would eventually turn over the responsibility for rocket launching, or at least a major share of it, to private business.

This effort was spearheaded by President Reagan, who, in May 1983, announced the government's support "in facilitating and encouraging commercial launch activities of ELVs (expendable launch vehicles) by the private sector." This policy applied to ELVs previously developed for government use as well as to new space launch systems developed specifically for commercial applications, and was consistent with the president's 1982 National Space Policy, which designates the space shuttle as the nation's primary space launch system.

To implement these important policy decisions, in November 1983, the president designated the Department of Transportation as the government's lead agency for administering commercial launch activities. This decision was followed by the formal signing, in February 1984, of Executive Order 12465, which "directed DOT to act as the focal point within the federal government for private sector space launch contacts."

Later in the year, Congress passed the Commercial Space Launch Act. The bill specified that:

1. The peaceful uses of outer space continue to be of great value and to offer benefits to mankind.

2. Private applications of space technology have achieved a significant level of commercial and economic activity, and

offer the potential for growth in the future, particularly in the United States.

3. New and innovative equipment and services are being sought, created, and offered by entrepreneurs in telecommunications, information services, and remote-sensing technology.

4. The private sector in the United States has the capability of developing and providing private satellite launching and associated services that would complement the launching and associated services now available from the United States government.

5. The development of launch vehicles and associated services on a commercial basis would enable the United States to retain its competitive position internationally, and contribute to the national interest and economic well-being of the United States.

Purposes of the new act were: "to promote economic growth and entrepreneurial activity through utilization of the space environment for peaceful purposes; and to encourage the United States private sector to provide launch vehicles and associated launch services by simplifying and expediting the issuance or transfer of launch licenses and by facilitating and encouraging the utilization of government-developed space technology."

In short, summed up U.S. senator Slade Gorton of Washington, chairman of the Senate's Subcommittee on Science, Technology, and Space, "This legislation seeks to facilitate private sector space launch activity by establishing the Department of Transportation as the lead federal agency with licensing authority over private expendable launch vehicle operations and by providing a framework within which this new industry can most effectively operate."

Senator Paul Trible of Virginia, one of the bill's chief

sponsors, added: "Exploiting the vast economic potential of space requires that the government be a partner, not an obstacle. The Commercial Space Launch Act is an important step, opening the final frontier of space to private enterprise."

Private industry hailed the new law, seeing it as an effective means to cut through what had previously been a forest of tangled government regulations. Said Fred Whiting, executive director of the American Space Foundation, a prospace citizens' lobby group with more than twenty-two thousand members: "Private commercial space launches [in the past] have been choked by an excess of bureaucratic red tape. In order to get a private ELV off the launch pad, the average firm has had to run a bureaucratic gauntlet of some eighteen federal agencies, overseeing twenty-two statutes or regulatory guidelines, none of them passed or promulgated with the express intent of overseeing commercial launch vehicles. . . . This act will release the bonds that have tied down American firms and have hampered them from competing effectively."

Donald ("Deke") Slayton, a former astronaut, and now president of Space Services, a private launch vehicle manufacturer, also praised the new legislation. "If the United States is to maintain its leadership position in space," he said, "the private sector must take advantage of the tremendous accomplishments of NASA, quickly developing a resource in space for the benefit of society."

Slayton and other experts pointed out, at congressional hearings preceding passage of the bill, that the United States already was losing ground to foreign nations who were getting into the space launch business. Principally, France's Ariane rocket has launched a large number of U.S. communications satellites into orbit, and other nations such as Japan and India are developing their own national launch systems.

By spring 1985, Arianespace, France's launching service, held firm orders for orbiting thirty satellites with options for twelve more, at a total cost of about $750 million. Half of the satellite customers were from outside of Europe, many from the United States.

Slayton also pointed out that he and others felt that private launches of rockets would not interfere with NASA's ongoing shuttle program. "We believe development of a commercial U.S. ELV industry will not conflict with the shuttle," he said. "The unique capabilities of the shuttle will maintain its position as an important space project. At the same time, we think an ELV industry can respond to market demand. A carefully crafted government policy can ensure that NASA and the private sector activities are complementary rather than competitive."

Slayton's company is but one of a growing number of firms that are getting into the space launch business. Here is a listing of a few of them:

• Space Services, of Houston, Texas, has developed a rocket called Conestoga, capable of boosting payloads up to 1,000 pounds (455 kg) into earth orbit for about $10 million a shot. The company's first test vehicle was successfully launched in September 1982. Possible missions could include the orbiting of satellites for earth remote sensing, search and rescue, low-earth-orbit communications, and materials processing.

• Two companies in the San Francisco, California, area— Starstruck and Pacific American Launch Systems—are working on development of new launch systems. Starstruck's primary objective is to build a rocket system called Constellation, to orbit communications satellites "for low cost and with high reliability." Pacific American is seeking funds for conceptual design of a system called Phoenix that could place payloads up to 15,000 pounds (6,804 kg) into orbit and recover the launch stages for further use.

• General Dynamics, which built the Atlas/Centaur launch vehicle for the Air Force, and Martin Marietta, which built the Titan, also for the Air Force, both are working on plans to develop these proven rocket systems for private flights. General Dynamics projects a strong commercial communications satellite market through the mid-1990s.

Both companies believe that their years of experience in launching spacecraft for the government, principally military satellites, gives them the edge over their competitors. This experience shows their dependability in the areas of launch scheduling and reliability of vehicles.

• Transpace Carriers, a new company located in Greenbelt, Maryland, also is interested in the lucrative communications satellite launch market. It proposes to fly modified versions of the Delta rocket, also initially developed for the U.S. Air Force. It also has a sound track-record, having launched more than 160 satellites into space for the government over the past quarter century.

Aside from booster rockets, other companies are interested in developing upper stages and other systems.

• Orbital Sciences Corporation, Washington, D.C., for example, is offering a transfer orbit state (TOS) for maneuvering commercial satellites and government payloads from a low earth orbit to high orbits, such as the geosynchronous orbit, 22,300 miles (35,900 km) up, necessary for communications satellites.

• McDonnell Douglas expects to sell about fifty of its commercially developed payload assist module (PAM-D) upper-stage systems by 1990. Already thirty-five have been sold. This vehicle is designed to place a payload of 2,750 pounds (1,250 kg) into geosynchronous orbit, on satellites that have been launched into lower earth orbit by ELVs or the space shuttle.

• Astrotech International Corporation, headquartered in Pittsburgh, Pennsylvania, is developing a "Delta Astrotech Transfer Stage," or DATS, that will be able to boost satellite payloads of up to 7,500 pounds (3,400 kg) from low-earth to higher orbits. Initial demand for such greater launch capability, the company believes, will come from both the military—for defense communications and missile early warning spacecraft—and from NASA, for scientific satellites. As the size of commercial satellites grows to take advantage of increased payload capacity, DATS will service this market as well.

• Fairchild Industries, of Germantown, Maryland, is working on development for a commercial "Leasecraft" satellite. It will provide a reusable space platform for private and government users who can benefit by in-orbit refurbishment or periodic return to earth of portions of the system. Leasecraft will supply essential power, command and data handling, and altitude control services to satellite payloads, and is designed for commercial space processing of metals, pharmaceuticals, and other potential products.

Still another way of making profits in space is envisioned by Commercial Cargo Spacelines of New York. It has signed a memorandum of understanding with NASA for chartering complete shuttle cargo bays, and has placed reservations with NASA for two launches in 1987. This company says it will offer users shuttle space for less than what they now have to pay the government, yet it believes it can produce revenues of $200 million a year.

And two firms, Astrotech International Corporation, and its subsidiary, the Space Shuttle of America Corporation, are seeking to buy from NASA an existing shuttle vehicle. From the sale of shares of stock in the company, the corporation also would build a shuttle and place in commercial operation two shuttle orbiters. Astrotech officials say such a venture would initiate revenue-generating commercial space transportation operations. They could market such a system more aggressively than can NASA and, they believe, bring in more space business.

At some point in the near future, possibly as early as the 1990s, it is likely NASA will turn over all launch responsibilities of the space shuttle to the highest bidders in private industry. This will occur, said former NASA head James M. Beggs, as soon as the shuttle is through its development phase and the flight rate is up to eighteen or twenty per year.

Otherwise, Beggs added, NASA would cease to be a research and development agency and instead become a high-tech trucking company. "We would be severely impacted by that kind of schedule," Beggs said. "We'd spend most of our time worrying about how to keep the flight rates up." To facilitate this transferal of launch responsibilities, NASA set up a Shuttle Strategic Planning Group which is developing a report on how to effect the switch to the private sector.

Still another potentially lucrative area for enterprising businesses will be in the storage and servicing of satellites, which to date has been largely handled by the U.S. government. Some experts have projected that as many as two hundred civilian commercial satellites will be launched within the next fifteen years at an estimated cost of $20 billion.

Already, Astrotech Space Operations, a division of the Astrotech International Corporation, has built a $7.5-million facility at a site adjacent to the launch pads at the Kennedy Space Center in Florida to store, process, and test satellites. Six spacecraft can be housed here at one time and three can be serviced simultaneously. Telesat of Canada became Astrotech's first paying customer when it stored its *Anik* communications satellite here in 1984 prior to launching.

All in all, the passage of the Commercial Space Launch Act by Congress has helped spur an onrush of interest from private companies which foresee the servicing and launching of payloads into orbit, and perhaps beyond, as a bright new business adventure whose time has come.

CHAPTER FIVE

GLOBAL COMMUNICATIONS

By far the most advanced area of space commercialization today is satellite communications. Although it has been hardly more than a quarter century since the first test spacecraft—*Echo 1*—was launched into earth orbit, successive generations of ever-increasingly sophisticated satellites, in that relatively short span of time, have revolutionized the way the world communicates.

These amazing electronic orbiters now provide, routinely, a master link for global transmission of voice, television, or high-speed data. And they provide more of it faster and at significantly less cost. Nearly 120 countries and territories on six continents regularly use communications satellites. It is possible today to reach nearly 250 countries and territories from almost any telephone in America. Twenty nations can be direct-dialed without operator assistance. More than one billion people—a fourth of the world's population—can witness an event as it happens via satellite television from space.

And unlike other areas of the developing space frontier,

which are still largely run, controlled, and funded by the federal government, spatial communications services are developed and operated by private companies like RCA, AT&T, Western Union, IBM, Hughes Aircraft, Aetna Life and Casualty Company, Communications Satellite Corporation, Ford Aerospace and Communications Corporation, and dozens of others.

Satellite communications has, in fact, become big business, with annual revenues estimated at anywhere from $12 billion to $15 billion. And this may be just the beginning of a continuing growth explosion for this dynamic new industry. With technologically advanced applications like data-relaying computers; direct broadcast satellites that will transmit television programs from space directly to small, inexpensive antennas; electronic mail; teleconferencing; and transmission to personalized, watch-sized receivers; experts believe the business will grow at a 25 percent annual rate through the rest of this century and beyond.

Al Parker, vice-president for marketing at Ford Aerospace and Communications Corporation, a leading manufacturer of satellites and telecommunications systems, says, "This is already a big business, and it is going to get much larger. How big is anybody's guess."

Even that great space visionary, Arthur C. Clarke, author of *2001: A Space Odyssey*, couldn't have foreseen such growth when, more than forty years ago, he published a concept of placing a ring of communications satellites in a geosynchronous earth orbit. Three such spacecraft, Clarke proposed, spaced equidistantly in stationary position, could cover the whole world, making possible a global radio communications system.

The theory of such a system is sound. For communications purposes, satellites offer unique advantages because they can overcome the "ground-bound" problems involved in spanning oceans and continents with submarine cables, land lines, and microwave radio stations for the long-distance transmission of radio, telephone, and television signals.

Because microwave travels in a straight line, relay stations, for example, must be spaced reasonably close to each other—about every 35 miles (56 km) or so—to allow for the earth's curvature so they can receive, amplify, and retransmit signals. To place stations this distance apart around the world would be prohibitively expensive. Similarly, submarine cables cost a lot to install and maintain, and generally have limited capacity.

One satellite, however, placed in a geosynchronous orbit 22,300 miles (35,903 km) above earth at the equator, can remain in a fixed position and provide communications relay coverage across an ocean to two or more continents. Three such satellites spaced at 120-degree intervals around the equator can effectively cover the entire globe, except for small areas around the North and South poles.

Realizing this potential, first proposed by Clarke, NASA began, in 1959, a program to develop the technology necessary to establish such a system. A year later, *Echo 1*'s passive radio reflector in space bounced signals from one point on the earth to another at up to intercontinental distances.

Then, on July 10, 1962, millions of television viewers in the United States and a few in France and England, watched a taped black and white picture of an American flag flapping in the New England breeze to the recorded accompaniment of "The Star Spangled Banner." Picture and sound, transmitted skyward over the Atlantic Ocean from a huge horn-shaped antenna near Andover, Maine, were transmitted to Andover and to Holmdel, New Jersey, from a new earth satellite—*Telstar 1*, built by the American Telephone and Telegraph Company and launched by NASA. *Telstar* signals also were picked up by ground stations in Europe. The space age of communications was effectively born. Two weeks later, mass audiences on both

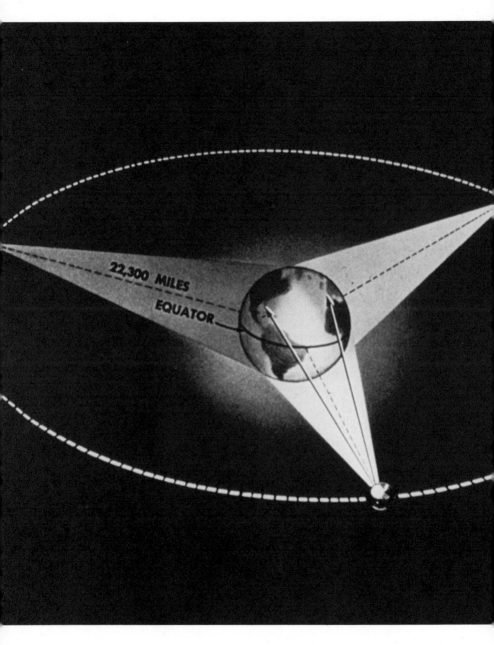

Diagram of a satellite in geosynchronous orbit

sides of the Atlantic watched the first international exchange of live television.

President John F. Kennedy, on August 31, 1962, signed Public Law 87-624—the Communications Satellite Act. "The ultimate result will be to encourage and facilitate world trade, education, entertainment, and many kinds of professional, political, and personal discourses which are essential to healthy human relationships and international understanding," Kennedy said.

Among other things, this act provided for the establishment of a new privately owned corporation to serve as America's entity in international satellite communications. Thus the groundwork was laid for the creation of the Communications Satellite Corporation, or Comsat.

By an act of Congress in February 1963, Comsat was given a charter to establish a commercial system "by itself, or in conjunction with other countries, but using investor funds." A year and a half later, the International Telecommunications Satellite Consortium—Intelsat—was formed, initially with fourteen nations, as a joint venture to establish the global commercial communications satellite system. Today, Intelsat is a partnership of organizations from more than one hundred nations. Comsat, now a privately owned U.S. company, serves as owner of the U.S. share of Intelsat satellites in addition to serving as manager of all the international satellites on behalf of all owners.

The first commercial communications satellite—*Early Bird 1*, or *Intelsat 1*—was launched on April 6, 1965, and was successfully placed in synchronous orbit over the Atlantic Ocean. "These satellites herald a new day in world communications," President Lyndon Johnson said at the time. "For telephone, message data, and television new pathways in the sky are being developed. They are sky trails to progress in commerce, business, trade, and in relationships and understanding among peoples."

Intelsat 1 had a capacity for handling 240 telephone conversations or one television program. In sharp contrast, each of today's series of Intelsats provides thirty-three thousand telephone channels, plus four color television channels simultaneously. The present system has a dozen or more operational and standby satellites interconnecting three hundred earth stations through a network of more than eight hundred links.

Today, satellite communications—telephone, television, data and facsimile transmission, and business transactions —have become an accepted necessity of everyday life. Here are some typical examples:

• Union Carbide, a large U.S. chemical company, reduced its long-distance telephone bill by nearly two thousand dollars a month by shifting its landline system to communications satellites. The company uses satellite transmission for teletype communications as well as voice transmission.

• RCA estimates that costs for transmitting via voice, data, facsimile, or teleprinter for only thirty to forty-five minutes daily, can be reduced up to 40 percent with use of satellite communications.

• The Holiday Inn reservation center in Chicago uses a privately leased satellite communications system to handle as many as 128,000 reservations a week. The cost savings are more than sixty thousand dollars annually.

• First Interstate Bank uses an American satellite to connect an electronic banking network of over seventy-five hundred terminals via satellite for on-line teller transaction processing, cash management, and automatic funds transfer. The network handles more than 750,000 transactions daily with an average response time of less than three seconds. The bank has saved over one million dollars in data communications costs in addition to increasing system use time and having nearly error-free processing.

Intelsat 5. *The Communications Satellite Corporation (Comsat) is the U.S. participant in Intelsat, an international cooperative of 110 nations that owns and operates the global commercial communications satellite system. As such, the corporation pioneered the first successful commercial venture in space—satellite communications. Through Intelsat, Comsat Corporation today transmits telephone conversations, television programming, and data and facsimile traffic to and from the United States. Each* Intelsat 5 *satellite has an average capacity of twelve thousand circuits and two television channels.*

• An American Express Company computer center in Phoenix uses a combination of satellites and phone links to approve 250,000 credit transactions a day from around the world, in an average of five seconds or less.

• A large insurance company routinely sends computerized material by satellite in twelve minutes. It would take thirty-one hours to transmit it by landlines.

• An RCA Americom communications satellite is being used to link hospitals on both coasts with a central computer complex near Chicago, providing turn-around times of ten minutes or less on electrocardiogram analysis.

• Atlantic Richfield Company has installed a $17-million video-teleconference system to connect by satellite its Los Angeles headquarters with offices in Philadelphia, Denver, Houston, Dallas, and Washington. Business executives can thus meet electronically and greatly reduce travel costs.

• Dow Jones and Company, publisher of the *Wall Street Journal*, uses a communications satellite to help publish its paper for subscribers in both the western and southeastern sections of the United States. Reproductions of each page are placed under a high-intensity light scanner that converts the black and white images into electronic impulses and beams them to the satellite. The satellite then beams these impulses back to publishing plants in different sections of the country for printing. Transmission of a full page takes only three and a half minutes. A number of other newspapers and magazines have followed this trend.

• The U.S. Postal Service is developing an international electronics postal system called Intelpost. Presently, half a dozen nations are involved, with mail-processing centers in Washington and New York, in Argentina, Canada, England, the Netherlands, and Switzerland. This system is expected to grow rapidly over the next few years with more countries entering and most countries extending their domestic service.

Communications satellites also blanket the world's oceans and have provided vast improvements for the shipping industry. Until just a few years ago, ships relied on traditional radio frequencies to communicate over long distances, using voice or Morse code, routing traffic through coastal radio stations operated by most maritime nations. Radio transmissions, however, are subject to frequent delays and disruptions, resulting from atmospheric or weather conditions.

According to one study, it takes four and a half to forty hours to send a typical telex message to a ship at sea, with an average delay of more than fifteen hours. To get a reply may take an additional thirty to forty hours. Thus, by this means it may take days for a shipowner to request urgent information from a ship and get an answer. By the time a shipowner got a message through, say to change course in midocean, it may cost him thousands of dollars, since operating costs for large ships are high.

That all changed with the introduction, in the mid-1970s, of Marisat satellites. This orbital network provides telephone, telex, facsimile services, high-speed data transmission, and distress or emergency communications. Today, the International Maritime Satellite Organization (Inmarsat)—a consortium of thirty-eight maritime nations chartered in 1979 and based in London—operates a fleet of geostationary satellites and earth coast-stations covering all three major ocean areas except the extreme polar regions.

The shipboard stations use 4-foot (122-cm) parabolic dish antennas, which are mounted on stabilized pedestals to keep them pointed toward the appropriate satellite as the ship rolls and pitches beneath it. With these in place, a ship at sea can be contacted via Inmarsat with full voice or telex communications in a matter of seconds, at any time of the day or night, regardless of the weather.

Although it was thought that domestic satellite systems would be used mostly for telephone trunking, two of their major applications have been for television program distribution to broadcasters and cable systems, and increasingly, for data transmission.

One of the fastest-growing areas is direct broadcast satellites. These are the satellites than can beam television programs to virtually any spot on earth, no matter how remote, that is equipped with a small, inexpensive antenna.

This concept was first proven in the mid-1970s when a satellite, positioned over Kenya, broadcast educational TV programs prepared by the Indian government to five thousand small villages all across India. Most of the inhabitants had never before seen a television image.

The potential commercial advantages of direct broadcast satellites are enormous. They will be able to reach millions of people in the United States and other nations who cannot receive cable TV. Antennas costing as little as two hundred dollars will pull in channels offering education, entertainment, and sports, for a small subscriber fee. Such systems are in operation in rural Japan and northwestern Canada, for example, where homes are so remote that conventional television systems are impossible.

Such firms as Time, Inc., Times Mirror Satellite Programming, Turner Broadcasting System, and Westinghouse Broadcasting System are spending millions of dollars to get in on the ground floor of direct broadcast satellites.

As the technology continues to expand, more and more applications are being considered and developed. One proposed concept is an educational television system that would interconnect sixty-five thousand U.S. schools and their sixteen thousand school district headquarters with color television and interactive audio channels, allowing students to ask or answer questions.

The system could also be used for four thousand universities and colleges, interconnected with 250,000 remote learning sites. Each school would be equipped with receive-only TV and two-way voice circuits. The schools would need only a small antenna 3 feet (91 cm) in diameter to receive the satellite signals.

Another promising development is electronic mail. Soon, letters will be sent from station to station via satellite. The message will be beamed to a satellite on a radio wave and relayed from there to a receiving station where the letter will be printed out and then delivered. Or the letter may be a direct copy of the original. Delivery of the mail will be faster, more reliable, and much less expensive.

Perhaps the most intriguing concept of all is a personal communications system, whereby individuals using a Dick Tracy–type wrist radio will be able to talk to anyone else anywhere in the country by satellite. Voice transmission would be sent by radio signal to orbit and bounced back to the receiver.

It will take satellites much larger than those in space today to make this happen. But, as *Science* magazine has reported, "the trend toward larger, more powerful and more complex satellites, smaller and less costly earth stations, and all-digital transmission systems is expected to continue through this century."

CHAPTER SIX

PROSPECTING FROM SPACE

Only in the past three or four decades has the human race finally begun to realize that the earth's rich resources, long thought to be inexhaustible, are, in fact, in very real danger of running out. The *Yearbook of Agriculture* had projected there will be six billion people on this planet by the year 2000. To feed the growing masses, experts say, food production must be doubled, yet arable land is decreasing annually.

During the last forty years, America alone has used more minerals and fuels than did the entire world in all of previous history. And the U.S. consumption of minerals is projected to double within the next twenty to twenty-five years. Drinking water, too, is expected to become much scarcer as the population soars.

All of this emphasizes how poorly earthlings have managed their planet's resources. A report by the Harvard University Center for Population a few years ago summed up the picture with this stark comment: "The 21st century may witness a world of half-starved, depressed human masses, gasping for air, short of sweet water, struggling to avoid one another, and living at a degraded subsistence level." And, warned Dr. William Pecora, former head of the United States Geological Survey: "If our ability to find and efficiently utilize resources does not accelerate, and accelerate rapidly, the industrial civilization we now enjoy will crumble within a few decades.

"The economic status of any nation is almost always a direct function of the use it makes of available natural resources," Dr. Pecora said. "Put in another way, natural resources are the nonhuman inputs to the economy, and economic growth results in large part from new discovery and effective use of these resources. If we had to depend on known supplies, we could predict collapse . . . in a couple of decades, and if we had to depend on supplies that could be found and developed, with present knowledge, disintegration would not long be postponed."

The irony of this is that there are plentiful life-sustaining supplies on the planet. In the world's oceans, which cover more than 70 percent of the globe . . . within the vast arctic tundra . . . and across enormous stretches of desert . . . in remote, nearly inaccessible mountain ranges . . . and in the crust and bowels of the earth . . . are great hordes of untapped resources.

There are mineral riches, energy sources, and food and water stores that far exceed the present and future needs of the world's billions of people. But these fresh supplies can support the ever-accelerating demands only if imaginative new ways are found to discover them effectively. New means, new tools must be developed to locate them.

The space age has provided such a means. The tools are satellites.

Laden with cameras capable of ultrahigh resolution and with sensitive measuring instruments, spacecraft in orbit several hundred miles up can take the earth's pulse electronically. They see what we cannot. Not only can they survey and inventory the world's resources far more economically and effectively than ever before, but they also can detect elusive clues that are leading to new supply sources.

This dawn of the new era of detecting, inventorying, and cataloging the earth's resources was launched July 23, 1972, when the first "earth resources technology satellite" was successfully placed in orbit. It was later named *Landsat 1*, and since then, four other satellites in the series have followed, the latest in 1984.

The Landsats travel in near-polar orbits, 570 miles (918 km) up, covering all earth latitudes between 80 degrees north and 80 degrees south. The orbital angle is set so that each satellite passes over every point under its path every eighteen days. This offers both broad and repetitive coverage.

Sophisticated spacecraft instrumentation works through a process known as remote sensing. That means the onboard equipment has the capability of detecting the nature of an object on earth without actually touching it. From space, sensors probe, or "listen to," an object electronically, then convert the electronic signals to a visual record—a photolike image.

Remote sensing is made possible by the simple physical fact that any object whose temperature is above absolute zero will reflect, transmit, emit, absord, or scatter protons— the basic units of electromagnetic energy. Across the visible and invisible spectra all objects yield distinctive "fingerprints," or spectral signatures, that are determined by the objects' atomic and molecular structures. Wheat, for example, has a different signature than corn or oats. Identification of these signatures also enables scientists to determine, not only what an object is, but how old and how healthy it is as well. The cell of a sick plant reflects or emits radiation differently than a healthy cell.

Remote sensing enables large areas, or those difficult to reach, to be surveyed in detail from space. In addition,

these surveys can be performed in minutes instead of the hours, days, or months that would be required for ground or air surveys of the same area.

Remote sensing and photographic data collected in space from Landsats, other satellites, and the space shuttle are supplied to the National Oceanic and Atmospheric Administration's Earth Resources Observation Systems (EROS) center in Sioux Falls, South Dakota. This data is in the public domain and copies may be purchased by anyone.

The center has millions of images from remote sensing stored, and has supplied hundreds of thousands of copies to private industry, individuals, state and local governments, academic and educational institutions, and foreign nations.

Users in private industry include Gulf Oil, Bechtel, Atlantic Richfield, Union Carbide, Mobile Oil, Texaco, Chevron, Continental Oil, Avco, Phillips Petroleum, and General Electric, among others. More than half of the 113 energy-related private companies in the United States have purchased data from EROS.

Federal government users include the Forest Service, Bureau of Land Management, Corps of Engineers, Department of State, Environmental Protection Agency, U.S. Geological Survey, and Department of Energy. More than one hundred nations now use Landsat data for resource evaluation and management.

The Landsat 5 *spacecraft undergoing a final*
check prior to launch at Vandenberg Air Force
Base, California, March 1984. Visible at
the top of the spacecraft is the Tracking and
Data Relay Satellite System (TDRSS) antenna.
When in space orbit this antenna is extended
12.5 feet (381 cm) above the spacecraft body.

Remote sensing from space represents the potential for a tremendously large new industry, which, within a few years, will be taken over by the private sector. To date, all launches and information sharing have been the responsibility of the U.S. government. But soon that will change, just as the communications satellite networks did.

And the market for such satellites and the data they uncover will be enormous. Consider some examples of how such capabilities will be used:

Agriculture. Satellites can photograph every sizable farm in the world to determine what crop is being raised and whether the crop is young or old, healthy or diseased, and accurately predict the yield. They can send advance warnings of droughts or even of changes in soil condition to help prevent blight. They can detect the larvae of insects such as the locust. Other agricultural uses can include analysis of the soil's moisture content, determination of irrigation requirements, and timely censuses of livestock.

Investigators using images of California's Imperial Valley taken from space inventoried in hours more than twenty-five separate crops in nearly nine thousand fields. The total area covered was almost half a million acres. They could even distinguish among wet planted fields, plowed lands, harvested fields, and bare soil in areas as small as ten acres.

Landsat 3 data in 1979 was used to revise government estimates of corn and soybean production. Satellites showed that original plant estimates made by conventional means were inaccurate for both crops—about 300,000 to 400,000 acres too high for corn.

Experts have used space images to obtain data needed to curb the boll worm in California; to track the dread Mediterranean fruit fly on the U.S. West Coast; and to survey destruction caused by the Dudaim melon, an inedible variety of cantaloupe that smothers cultivated crops. Mexico has used Landsat images to help eradicate the

Infrared photo taken in one of the first experiments in identification of corn blight. In the original infrared photo of Indiana cornfields, healthy corn showed up as bright red, dead or dying leaves photographed much darker.

screwworm, which causes annual losses to cattle and poultry in the hundreds of millions of dollars.

Forestry. The U.S. Forest Service keeps a continuing inventory of the country's timber in order to be able to provide statistics on volume, growth, and drain to local and national planners and legislators. Yet, some information is as much as nine years old when reported, because of the difficulties and cost of collecting information about woodlands.

To foresters, a satellite system is the only practical way to mount a constant watch over vast wooded areas to provide warning of insect infestations and diseased trees, take censuses of trees, and report logging yields. Instruments in space can spot forest fires burning in remote places.

By using Landsat, it has been found that identification of timber type can be as high as 95 percent accurate and identification of condition as high as 80 percent accurate. This contributes significantly to the capability of pinpointing available timber supplies in terms of location, type, quality, and quantity.

The Saint Regis Paper Company, for example, uses two satellites to monitor two and a half million acres of company land in Alabama, Florida, Georgia, Louisiana, Mississippi, and Texas. Other paper and timber companies also use Landsats to measure their forests and are increasingly using them to monitor the condition of the trees.

Geology. New mineral and energy sources, unknown and unseen by people on earth, can be spotted with ease from space. Most metallic mineral deposits and subterranean gas and oil stores are associated with such earth structures as rock folds and faults. Prospecting from space permits charting of known resource areas and discovery of new ones in remote areas. While it is impossible for them actually to detect minerals, space satellites can help locate areas that look promising because of their large structure features.

Geologists can then investigate those areas through aerial photography.

Geologists using a new system of enhanced imagery developed by General Electric, which pinpoints lineaments, anomalies, and structural features with currently known geologic formations, were able to predict eleven potential oil-drilling locations, and all eleven areas produced wells.

Imagery from space of subsurface features has revealed ancient terrain of previously unknown river systems as large as the Nile buried beneath the desert sands of southern Egypt and northern Sudan.

Hydrology. Satellite imagery is being used to inventory water in regional basins by measurement of lake levels, river flow rates, irrigation patterns, and drainage patterns. Satellites also provide early warning of floods by monitoring rainfall and surveying drainage basins. They locate aquifers and determine the suitability of various sites for constructing dams and storing water. And Landsats estimate water resources through snow and frozen water surveys, and determine the location of seepage and other ground water sources.

Oceanography. The world's oceans are our greatest and least-used natural resources. Covering over 133 million square miles (344 million sq km) of the planet, this very vastness has made it impractical to undertake continual broad-scale surveillance of them by conventional means. The job can be done effectively with satellites. Infrared instruments from orbital platforms can be used to trace the temperature outlines of ocean currents and upwellings, and can help lead the way to one of our major food supplies—fish. Surface temperatures can help identify the highest concentrations of plankton—the prime source of food for fish. An early Landsat proved this by leading Taiwanese fishermen to an area previously undiscovered, but teeming with edible marine life.

This image of Memphis, Tennessee, was received
from the Landsat 4 spacecraft thematic mapper on
August 22, 1982, from approximately 450 miles
(725 km) above the earth. The changing course
of the Mississippi in times of flood is charted on the
image as a confusion of dry oxbows. The city of
West Memphis is discernible to the left of the river.

Satellite data also is being used as a means to monitor such oceanographic features as sea conditions, distribution of sea ice, surface temperatures, current patterns, and biological developments. This provides information vital to the shipping industry.

Landsat data also is being used extensively for such diverse uses as pollution control, soil evaluation, climate study, wildlife management, cartography, and earthquake detection. In fact, the potential for remote sensing of the earth from space is virtually limitless.

In general, earth orbital photography provides surveys of large areas and isolated sections that would require a tremendous amount of time if done by conventional means; in some cases it would be extremely difficult or even impossible to make the survey on the ground.

One Landsat satellite, however, takes a picture of the earth every twenty-five seconds. Each of those pictures covers an area 115 miles by 115 miles (185 km). To do this by aerial photography would cost more than $100,000—billions of dollars to cover the entire earth.

Already, more than forty commercial companies are involved in the business of enhancing, analyzing, and interpreting Landsat and weather satellite data, creating a multimillion-dollar industry.

Geoscience and Services, of Fort Worth, Texas, for example, began operations in 1982, and its business has grown steadily, especially in image interpretation and consulting, which includes recommendations of where to lease property for petroleum exploration and where to drill. "Very few people understand the Landsat data well enough to make the images worthwhile to them," says Geoscience president Velon Minshew.

The Center for Space Policy, a Cambridge, Massachusetts, "think tank," has forecast that gross revenues from remote sensing might reach $2 billion annually by the year 2000 for raw data sales alone, with another $2 billion projected for the translation of such data into intelligible forms.

Charles Sheffield, vice-president for special projects at Earth Satellite Corporation in Chevy Chase, Maryland, has said that the demand for earth resources and environmental data—heretofore collected by space-based sensors launched and operated by the U.S. government—will reach the point, possibly by the early 1990s, where it will be a profitable business for the private sector.

The U.S. government is no longer in the remote-sensing launch business. Its last flight was *Landsat 5*. However, it is only a matter of time before this operation will be assumed by commercial enterprises. Even now, a group of companies known as Space America has announced plans for a private satellite service for farmers and mineral companies worldwide. An initial satellite is scheduled to be launched in the late 1980s. Eventually, three satellites in polar orbit are planned. They would provide fresh data over each area covered every five to six days.

Geospectra Corporation, in Ann Arbor, Michigan, is in the process of forming a partnership of about ten mining and petroleum companies to design, launch, and operate a geological remote-sensing satellite they will call Geostar.

There is some controversy, however, over just how and when private enterprise will take over the government's role in launching future Landsats. The groundwork for private takeover of this responsibility from NASA was laid in 1984 with passage of the Land Remote Sensing Commercialization Act. Under this law, Landsat was supposed to become a private operation over a period of six years.

But the transference has been delayed. Initially, seven companies bid on the contract and this field was eventually narrowed to the Earth Observing Satellite Company (Eosat), a joint venture by RCA's Astro Electronics Division and the Hughes Aircraft Company. The problem centers on how much the government should subsidize Eosat to get the program started. The Reagan administration has imposed a $250-million ceiling, which most industry observers be-lieve is too little. Experts feel it would require too much investment and represent too much risk for any one com-pany to undertake the project at this time. Negotiations are continuing between the government and Eosat.

Meanwhile, the French, too, have intentions to launch remote-sensing satellites, and Japan's Space Council is studying the feasibility of launching sixteen land and ocean observation spacecraft before the year 2000. They are primarily interested in ocean monitoring since major ele-ments of their economy and health are linked to the sea. They also plan to use the data to help predict earthquakes, volcanic activity, and tidal waves.

Despite the current problems with governmental red tape in the United States, the day is fast approaching when the United States will enter the commercial remote-sensing satellite business in a big way. The fantastic successes of Landsat have paved the way toward the birth of a whole new industry—prospecting from space.

In future years, this venture will be run entirely by private companies which will build and launch the satellites, build and operate the sensing equipment, and then analyze, interpret, and distribute the information to eager users all over the world. And we will, at last, find the means to properly manage the earth's precious resources.

CHAPTER SEVEN

DOWN-TO-EARTH BENEFITS

The major thrust of the commercialization of space is centering, understandably, on activities *in* space—everything from communications satellites to minifactories in earth orbit—or on the means to reach space, via a variety of launch vehicles and transportation systems.

Amidst all of this activity, hundreds of private companies are, and have been for some time, marketing thousands of products manufactured and serviced on the ground, by using technologies spawned by the national space effort.

"By their challenging nature, NASA programs are particularly demanding of technological input," explained Ronald J. Philips, director of NASA's Technology Utilization and Industry Affairs Division, in *Space Spinoff 1984.* "Meeting the aeronautical and space research goals of the past quarter century has necessitated advancements across a diverse spectrum that embraces virtually every scientific and technological discipline.

"Much of the hardware developed to meet program needs, having served its purpose, is no longer extant,"

Philips said. "But the technology remains. It is a national resource, a bank of knowledge available for application to new products and processes of benefit to the national economy, industrial efficiency, and human welfare.

"This ever-expanding storehouse of technical knowledge has been well utilized over the past two decades or more. NASA's own efforts to reapply the technology, and those of imaginative entrepreneurs, have generated thousands of secondary applications—'spinoffs'—spanning a broad range of public needs and conveniences," continued Philips.

"It is difficult to find a facet of everyday life wherein spinoff has not pervaded. NASA technology has been transferred to the fields of medicine, public safety, transportation, industrial processes, pollution control, energy systems, construction, law enforcement, home appliances, farm machinery, sports and recreation, food products—the list can be expanded to catalog length. Collectively, these innovations represent a valuable contribution to American employment, productivity, and life-style."

And, as the shuttle flights continue to smooth the highway to orbit, more and more spinoffs are being generated on earth. Some of the most visible are in the field of medicine.

Intec Systems of Pittsburgh, Pennsylvania, for example, produces a pocket-sized device called AID-B, which is a human-implantable heart assist system that reportedly helps save thousands of lives a year. Based on technology first developed for miniaturized space circuitry, AID-B detects erratic heart actions, known as arrhythmias, and delivers a corrective electrical countershock to restore rhythmic heartbeat.

Lifecycle, an Irvine, California, company, markets a sensing electrode device that monitors the heart rate of exercisers to ensure that they stay within healthy limits during strenuous workouts. The concept was first used, more than a decade ago, to check heart rates of astronauts over long periods of time.

Ingestible toothpaste, also developed for astronauts on space flights, now is being marketed commercially by Scherer Laboratories, of Dallas, Texas. It is an important aid to maintaining oral hygiene among bedridden patients in hospitals, nursing homes, and other special-care facilities.

Other space-spawned medically related products and systems range from special devices for paraplegics to electronic patient monitoring devices in hospitals, and from biological isolation garments patterned after astronaut suits, to revolutionary accelerometers which measure minute muscular tremors in the human body.

Applications in other fields are equally innovative. Shane Associates of Wynnewood, Pennsylvania, now produces an anticorrosive protective coating that lasts years longer than previous products. It resulted from NASA studies aimed at protecting its launch towers at the Kennedy Space Center in Florida from the ravages of salt air and spray and from the fiery exhaust flames of rising rockets.

Hohman Plating and Manufacturing, in Dayton, Ohio, is marketing a product called Surf-Kote C-800, a self-lubricating metal-glass-fluoride coating that resists oxidation at temperatures up to 1,600° Fahrenheit (870° C). Initially developed for missile and space uses, it now protects sliding contact bearings, shaft seals for turbopumps, piston rings for high performance compressors, and hot-glass-processing machinery.

Advanced Refractory Technologies, of Buffalo, New York, uses space age technology to produce specialty ceramic powders, which help increase industrial productivity, lower energy usage, and reduce demand for scarce raw materials.

Dodge Products, of Houston, Texas, markets a line of solar energy sensing, measuring, and recording devices that incorporate solar cell technology first refined for space applications by NASA. Commercial customers include architects, engineers, and others engaged in construction and operation of solar energy facilities; manufacturers of solar cell systems or solar-related products, such as glare-reducing windows; and others.

NASA's Johnson Space Center conducted research for years on advanced flame-resistant materials in an effort to reduce fire hazards in the space shuttle. A polyimide foam was found to resist ignition better than any material used earlier. Imi-Tech Corporation, in Elk Grove Village, Illinois, now sells this product for use in acoustical treatments of doors, walls, and ceilings, and as thermal insulation.

Manufactured by Hitco Materials Division of Armco, of Gardenia, California, a ceramic fiber insulation material known as Refrasil has been used extensively as a heat-absorbing ablative reinforcement for such space systems as rocket motor nozzles and reentry shields. It can withstand temperatures of 3,000° Fahrenheit (1,648° C), and has found a number of industrial high temperature applications where glass, asbestos, and other materials fail.

Chesebrough-Pond's, Greenwich, Connecticut, is using NASA technology to monitor ten thousand electric motors in the company's thirty-two plants across the country. The device, an inexpensive, computerized motor controller, regulates the motors' output and dramatically reduces the energy they use.

Space age spinoffs have even helped improve hair styling techniques. Hair styling equipment, using heat, can cause cracks, blisters, or pinching of hair fiber if it is defective. By using technology first funded by NASA, Redkin Laboratories, Canoga Park, California, has developed a new line of styling appliances that use a heat-sensing device to prevent malfunction.

Foster Grant Corporation, Leominster, Massachusetts, has used NASA research to perfect a highly abrasion-resistant coating for the plastic lenses of its product line of sunglasses.

The list goes on and on—electronic weight control systems for highway trucking; tires made safer through use of an ultrasensitive fast-scanning infrared optical device;

new, advanced aircraft control systems; flame-resistant foams; antifogging compounds for clearer windshields; rescue search beacons; freeze-dried foods; thermal cooking pins; long-lasting nickel-cadmium batteries; flat electrical wiring; new metallic alloys.

These and hundreds of other devices and systems—all fostered by the new technologies needed to send humans and machines into space—are being developed, manufactured, and marketed throughout the United States and the world today to improve and make more convenient our way of life. And with this transference of benefits from space to the ground has come a vast new array of companies employing thousands of people to make profits here on earth.

CHAPTER EIGHT

THE ORBITAL FACTORY

Within the next few years, experiments now being carried out on shuttle flights will lead the way to the creation of a whole new industry—orbital manufacturing. The concept is not new. The Skylab series of missions in the early 1970s proved, in a laboratory setting, the feasibility of producing items as diverse as metals and crystals. Larger and more sophisticated tests on shuttle flights are broadening the realm of possibilities.

Such experimentation is confirming the fact, long theorized, that certain manufacturing processes can be done better in the absence of gravitational fields, or in a vacuum which space offers. Materials that will not mix on earth—oil and water, certain metals—will mix in space. This space manufacturing could lead to: the production of new and vastly improved products; more precise manufacturing of products; and new materials-processing techniques.

The development of metal foam could be one future example. Space promises the production of stable foams from a wide variety of liquefied materials and gases. Consequently, it is conceivable that a foamed steel having the weight of balsa wood, but retaining many properties of solid steel, could be made. Such a process is impossible on earth because the weight of the liquid metal causes the gas foam bubbles to rise to the surface before cooling can take place. In a weightless atmosphere, gases will remain entrapped and produce a spongelike material.

Similar techniques can be used to mix materials of such different densities and properties as steel and glass. Composite and foamed materials should yield lighter and stronger material for basic study, probable industrial applications, and even future spacecraft construction.

Glass manufacturers say ultrapure products such as high-quality lenses for lasers and optical instruments will be produced much more easily in space because impurities in production caused by the need for containers on earth will be eliminated. In gravity-free orbit, no containers will be necessary.

Single crystals grown on earth are limited in size by outside forces or contaminants. In an immaculate zero-gravity space environment, there are no limits to potential growth. Oversize crystals, grown of the right material and with the proper impurities controlled, could be used as very large power transistors, and if they are pure quartz, as optical blanks for near-perfect lenses.

Crystals are also employed in such applications as computer memories; optical communications; lasers; photovoltaic cells used for solar electric power; optoelectronics; and a multitude of instruments used for pyroelectric detection, surface acoustics, and ultrasonics. Glass crystals not obtainable in conventional silicate, borate, and phosphate-based glasses can be obtainable in space for advanced optical systems and laser uses. Further examples of products made from glass crystals that can be produced better in space include large silicon crystals, silicon ribbon, fiber optics, film memories, integrated circuit chips, space glass

Shown here is a model of an industrial space facility. This concept includes two hollow center modules which are habitable. Docking ports are at the end and center of the modules. The small module at the top of each cylinder is a supply module which is removable. Two solar panels extend from each side of the large modules.

amorphous semiconductors, and semiconducting glass and solar cells.

Another aspect of space materials-processing that intrigues scientists and engineers is levitation melting. Suspending a specimen in air (levitation)—or in this case, in space—is important because it creates the possibility of melting materials without contamination. Metallic materials and structures can be shaped by the manipulation of surrounding electromagnetic fields with resulting perfect shapes. The virtual absence of gravitational forces makes this a natural process for space application.

This is impossible on the earth, for the conditions of gravity require more current to levitate the material than is needed to melt it, and it cannot be cooled unless it rests on something. In space, however, metallic material is easily levitated and held in place, and the current can be increased for softening or melting. Manipulation of the magnetic fields in a coil system permits the specimen to be moved about without its touching anything. It can be melted and resolidified, therefore, without becoming contaminated or deformed.

Such a method would permit production of perfect spheres for use as ball bearings that would launch a new order of mobility for wheels. Uniform alloys could be produced because maximum intermixing of constituents is possible, as would be the refinement of metals to high levels of purity.

High-gravity metals and semiconductors, such as tungsten, are desirable for X-ray tubes, and beryllium is needed for neutron spectrometers. These materials are readily contaminated by their containers in the earth's gravity. In space, no such problem would exist. Similarly, porous metallic structures tend to collapse under the gravitational stresses of the earth, but would not in orbit. These structures, formed of materials that melt at high temperatures and have unique properties, are produced by mixing the components together and heating them to a temperature high enough to fuse them, but not to melt and intermix them. This process, called sintering, is used to produce porous bearings and filters, metallic frictional materials, abrasive tools, electric lamp filaments, some electric contacts, motor and dynamo brushes, and a variety of soft and hard magnetic materials.

In metallurgy, examples of products that experts believe can be made better and more efficiently in space include magnets, catalysts, superconductors, electrical contact material, bearing alloys, jewelry, solid lubricants, turbine blades, thermoelectrics, metal fibers, foam metals, fiber-reinforced metals, and high-purity refractory materials.

There are many other advantages of manufacturing products in space factories. Experts say machinery used in orbit would virtually never wear out. Without the physical constraints of gravity, workers and equipment would move about effortlessly. The individual productivity of workers would increase sharply because of the lower amounts of energy expended. Such negative side effects of earthbound production as pollution, congestion, and industrial accidents could be all but eliminated.

It is not surprising then that a number of America's leading manufacturing corporations, such as General Motors, 3-M, Grumman Aerospace Corporation, and John Deere, along with many other companies are leading the way toward this new industrial revolution by committing hundreds of millions of dollars in research and development programs.

And the potential payoff could be enormous. The Center for Space Policy, an organization in Cambridge, Massachusetts, that specializes in evaluating commercial and industrial opportunities in space, forecasts that by the year 2000 annual revenues from space-processed glasses alone could reach more than a billion dollars, and gallium arsenide semiconductor processing could bring in another three billion-plus a year. Rockwell International, one of the nation's leading aerospace contractors and the builder of the space shuttle, has prepared a detailed report that pro-

The Long Duration Exposure Facility (LDEF) high above the Gulf of Mexico. The LDEF weighs 22,000 pounds (10 t) and carries fifty-seven experiments for universities and private industries from the United States and eight other countries.

jects a $6-billion electronic materials market annually as early as the 1990s.

Although it will still be several years before earth-bound companies can realize actual profits from orbital manufacturing, NASA's new space commercialization policy has been carefully drawn up to encourage investment from the private sector. Federal tax monies derived from space ventures may even be recycled as "seed money" to motivate more companies to move into the arena of space, and arrangements are being made for the government to purchase some of the products made in orbit.

One of the first companies to seriously consider manufacturing in space, somewhat surprisingly, was John Deere. It is surprising because Deere is a world leader in the production of farm equipment. In 1981, Deere became the first private company to sign a technical-exchange agreement with NASA, which permitted the firm to perform cast-iron solidification experiments on board conventional NASA aircraft, which can be flown to simulate gravity-free conditions for thirty to sixty seconds. Deere since has signed a memorandum of understanding with NASA to cooperate on the design of metallurgical tests to be conducted aboard space shuttle flights.

Deere is funding such advanced research in hopes of improving its massive iron foundry operations, and the service life of metal components in its tractors, combines, and other machinery. For example, Deere produces about 600 million pounds (273 million kg) of cast iron per year. One objective of the space experimentation is to observe the cooling and solidification of molten iron in the weightlessness of space to obtain a better understanding of the process so that new data can be applied to foundry operations on the earth to reduce costs and improve the metal produced. NASA is granting Deere free transportation costs on the shuttle because it believes such information will have applications to all U.S. foundry operations.

Another result of the testing will be to determine if it would be possible, and practical, to manufacture iron-carbon composite materials in space. The alignment of the graphite structures in these materials could enable the material to have higher thermal conductivity and strength in the direction of a heat flow with lower conductivity. If this can be done effectively, it is conceivable Deere and others would manufacture certain elements of their product line in orbit. Deere is reviewing its shuttle experiment concepts with Bethlehem Steel, and with several universities.

The 3M Corporation, a diversified multibillion-dollar manufacturing company, also has embarked on an aggressive long-term research program to discover new materials and processes. The company is investigating the future possibility of breakthroughs that would lead to a faster generation of light-powered electrooptical data processing and storage systems. This could greatly advance the U.S. electronics and computer industries.

NASA and 3M have entered into a ten-year joint endeavor agreement designed not only to allow free company experiment space on shuttle flights, but also to transfer these activities into a permanent space station when it is constructed. With an aim toward eventual production of commercial products in orbit, initial 3M projects involve organic crystalline materials, and the preparation of thin film that could have applications in the fields of electronics, energy conservation, and biology. The advances made in organic chemistry in space has 3M researchers excited. They offer the potential of millions of new compositions, many of which are important to advanced data processing and image or sensor sensitivity.

"Organic chemistry is one of the most lucrative areas you could envision and leads to a variety of different products with different properties," says Christopher Podsiadly, director of 3M's science research laboratory. "We would like to study these on the molecular level, such as on films and other surfaces. The key is to investigate them systematically in a long-term basic research program in space. Then I can guarantee we will be commercializing new products based on that research." Under terms of the agreement with NASA, it is likely that 3M scientists will fly on future shuttle flights.

Grumman Aerospace Corporation, of Bethpage, New York, also is committing resources to gather basic data on how materials and processes are affected by the space environment. Experiments developed for three shuttle flights have concentrated on use of a furnace system to determine whether complex convection and turbulence in liquid metal flows pose a problem to the experiment improving the metal's final properties. Bismuth and manganese-bismuth alloys were selected for the initial flight, and samarium and cobalt were used later. Results of the tests—designed to improve the materials' coefficient of resistance to demagnetization and learn the effects of the manned shuttle environment on the solidification process—are now being studied.

One company, Microgravity Research Associates, of Coral Gables, Florida, is seeking funds to finance the commercial production of gallium arsenide semiconductor crystals in space. The company believes this market will exceed $100 billion annually within the next two decades.

Gallium arsenide has properties far superior to silicon, which has been the basic electronics industry semiconductor material for several decades. Richard Randolph, Microgravity president, believes supercomputers that will perform billions of computations every second, stategic defense systems, and advanced satellite communications systems will have requirements that will surpass the present technological capabilities of silicon. This, he feels, will open the market for new semiconductor materials.

In an agreement with NASA, Microgravity Research Associates will develop and provide the flight hardware to grow gallium arsenide crystals in shuttle payloads. NASA will orbit the company's gallium arsenide furnace on seven or eight flights, after which the company must commit to commercialize its crystals in space.

Another company, Microgravity Technologies, of San Diego, California, is developing plans to produce gallium arsenide, cadmium telluride, and indium phosphide semiconductors in orbit. This company expects to produce not only semiconductor materials, but also laser and fiber-optic glasses, and to design instruments and equipment that will be used in space processing. They are working with NASA on a joint endeavor agreement for use of the shuttle.

The Special Metals division of Astrotech International Corporation, Pittsburgh, Pennsylvania, is the world's leading producer of space age superalloys for use in the high heat and stress environment of jet engines. As part of its efforts to remain in the vanguard of superalloy technology, Special Metals is working with NASA and several universities to complete the details of an experiment on the solidification of alloys in the zero gravity of space. The experiment will be performed on a future space shuttle mission. It is expected to provide valuable technical information that the division will use to create even more technically complex materials and improve the production processes for existing alloys.

As the day of the reality of a permanent space station nears, more and more U.S. and foreign corporations are turning their attention, and their research resources, to the ever-brightening prospects of manufacturing products in orbit.

NASA is continuing to encourage this transition, and is developing a growing storehouse of science and technology to process materials in space. This data is being made available to private industry, a policy that should help reduce the large financial risk needed to launch company efforts in orbit.

Says Robert Naumann of the space science laboratory at NASA's Marshall Space Flight Center in Huntsville, Alabama: "If the customer [private industry] can use government equipment and take advantage of the steps the government has taken, such as using the technology or equipment we've already developed, it reduces both the risk and time of [financial] return. It is not unlike the government funding basic research in atomic energy."

Such encouragement, added to the positive in-space processing experiments that are being carried out today aboard the shuttle, will lead soon to what one aerospace publication has called "the gold rush in outer space."

CHAPTER NINE

PHARMACIES
IN SPACE

To date, the field of medicine has been one of the chief beneficiaries of the onrush of technology spawned by the space age. The range of spinoffs that already are being applied on earth covers a broad spectrum. As impressive as they are, however, they seem minor to what is projected for the immediate future.

Experts are predicting that advances in medical processing techniques expected over the next few years will not only lead to a multibillion-dollar annual business, but also will open new treatment methods that promise cures for such dreaded diseases as cancer, diabetes, and malaria, among others.

Space provides a pure environment, and the zero gravity of earth orbit will enable specialists to separate materials they are unable to separate economically on earth.

For example, scientists have determined that it may be possible to develop new cures or improved treatments for many diseases by using cells, enzymes, hormones, or proteins produced by the human body. On the earth, these substances are separated from biological materials by a process called electrophoresis—but because the earth's gravity exerts a negative influence on the separation process, only a tiny amount of sample can be extracted at one time. Processing in gravity-free space offers a means of separating biologicals in the large quantities and high levels of purity needed for pharmaceutical production.

This is possible because the electrophoresis method separates biological materials, such as human cells, by means of an electrical field (electrical voltage force). When this is done on earth, sedimentation is a problem if the particles to be separated are large and heavy, since the gravitational force on the particles becomes large relative to the electrophoresis forces. Also, convection—the upward movement of a gas or liquid that is cooled—causes currents that tend to remix the separate factions. In space, sedimentation and convection are virtually absent. Cells in orbit will separate because each cell reacts in a different degree to the electrical field.

Once such processes are perfected, new vaccines and drugs can be produced in volumes that could aid millions of people. Some potential applications:

• Mass production of beta cells could provide a single-injection cure for diabetes. On the ground, restricted by the earth's gravity, it is impossible to isolate enough beta cells to treat even a few patients. There is no reason that large, commercially viable amounts of beta cells cannot be made in orbit. If this capability is proven, it could help more than three million sufferers of diabetes.

• Interferon is considered important for providing the body with immunity from viral infections, and is being studied as a treatment for cancer. While earth-based processing of interferon can provide only low yields and low purity, space offers the dual promise of high yields and high purity. The annual patient load that could benefit is twenty million people.

• More than one million people a year would gain from space-based processing of products that stimulate epidermal growth, important in treating burn patients and in the healing of wounds. On the earth, only research quantities of low purity are possible.

• The same is true of growth hormone products that can stimulate juvenile bone growth in patients with deficiencies that threaten the length and quality of life. Such hormones also promote the healing of ulcers. If large quantities of these growth hormone products can be made in orbit, as projected by scientists, they can benefit 850,000 people annually.

• Up to half a million patients could be aided if antitrypsin products can be mass-produced in space. These would limit the progress of emphysema and enhance cancer chemotherapy.

• Antihemophilic products manufactured on earth are of generally low purity and sometimes cause harmful side effects. If made in space, they could eliminate immunological reactions (blood disorders) for as many as fifteen thousand people.

In fact, the theory of space processing of medical products was proved in 1975 during the Apollo-Soyuz joint United States–Soviet space flight. On that historic mission, kidney cells and lymphocytes (white blood cells) were successfully separated in orbit. The kidney cells were processed to isolate pure urokinase—the only natural substance known to be effective in dissolving blood clots.

Production of large quantities of urokinase outside the

human body, for use in treating heart attacks, strokes, and phlebitis (inflammation of a vein or veins) is difficult because of the large amounts of urine required to obtain urokinase on earth. On the Apollo-Soyuz flight, the kidney cells separated in space produced six to seven times more urokinase than would have been possible on earth.

The lymphocyte separation in space in 1975 was part of the research into the human immune system that studied, for instance, why certain people are subject to cancer. In preparing the lymphocytes on earth for the flight, a new freezing method was found that could preserve the lymphocytes for as long as five years. That meant it would no longer be necessary for leukemia patients to depend on the immediate availability of relatives to provide needed blood transfusions. The transfusions may now be stored.

Armed with such confirmations that the space processing of medical products is achievable, researchers eagerly awaited the advent of the space shuttle system when more and larger projects and products could be tested and proven.

One of the first of these occurred on the third shuttle flight, which began March 22, 1982. A monodisperse latex reactor experiment produced tiny plastic spheres made of polystyrene, a chemical product—which may have major medical and industrial applications—successfully as planned. On the earth, production of such spheres is severely limited by gravity-caused convection.

The reactor has flown on several shuttle missions to date, resulting in the accumulation of hundreds of millions of the minuscule spheres. The National Bureau of Standards, an agency of the Department of Commerce, began offering the microscope latex spheres for sale in 1985 as the "first commercial space product." Packages containing twenty-seven million spheres—enough to fill a teaspoon—are being sold to laboratories for calibrating powerful electron microscopes and for other research purposes. Price per package is approximately $350.

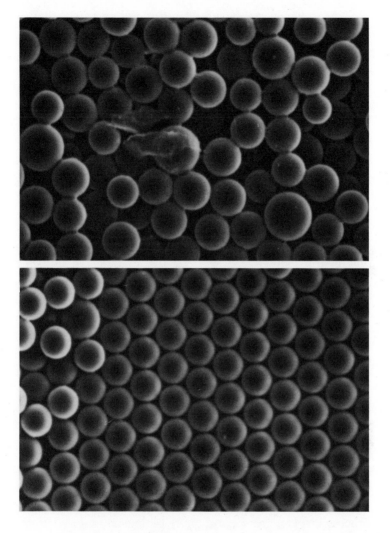

Particles made in the low-gravity environment of space grow uniformly in size and shape. The photograph at the top shows 10-micrometer polystyrene spheres made on Earth. Below, the same chemical process used in space produces a superior calibration material.

The spheres can be used as tiny rulers to determine relative sizes of objects under microscopes, and to calibrate filters, particle counters, and porous membranes.

Possible future applications for the spheres include calibrating the pores in human intestines in cancer research, and the human eye in glaucoma research, and use as carriers of drugs and radioactive isotopes for treatment of cancerous tumors. If there is a major difference in pores within healthy and tumorous cells, then the latex microspheres could become missiles that would stick inside tumors but not healthy tissues, thus carrying a higher drug dose in malignant tissues.

One of the nation's first major-sized corporations to commit its resources to the future development of medicines and pharmaceuticals in space is the McDonnell Douglas Astronautics Company in Saint Louis, Missouri. McDonnell Douglas entered into a joint endeavor agreement with NASA in which NASA provides shuttle flight time for company-developed experiments under a policy designed to encourage private investment in space industrialization.

McDonnell Douglas and its partner—Ortho Pharmaceutical Corporation, a division of Johnson and Johnson—are exploring the commercial feasibility of space-processed pharmaceuticals. To date, the two companies have spent tens of millions of dollars over the last several years in this intense research effort.

One of the most visible results has been the development of a "continuous flow electrophoresis system" (CFES) that has been tested on a number of shuttle flights. This process involves the separation of biological material from its surrounding medium by passing a fluid between walls across which an electric charge has been established.

On the fourth shuttle flight, in November 1982, the CFES processed about five hundred times more biological material in the weightlessness of space than could be achieved on the ground. On the sixth flight, in June 1983, seven hundred times more biological material was processed with four times the purity that could be attained on earth.

In September 1985, after years of research work and the expenditure of millions of dollars, Ortho announced it was canceling its space program for the orbital production of this product. The company stated that advances in genetic engineering on earth made it possible to produce the hormone more quickly in normal gravity under controlled laboratory conditions.

While this was a disappointment, McDonnell Douglas said it remained confident it would find another partner to continue its experiments in this product area.

In fact, if continuing research confirms the practicability and profitability of commercial pharmaceutical processing, McDonnell Douglas plans to start production in an unmanned earth-orbiting facility. This space factory would operate continuously for months at a time, serviced by shuttle crews who would periodically deliver raw materials and collect separated products.

McDonnell Douglas is working on a different project with the Washington University School of Medicine in Saint Louis. The company and the university have signed a fifteen-year joint research agreement to pursue new treatments for diabetes. In tests with laboratory animals on earth, Washington University researchers have successfully controlled diabetes by implanting live, insulin-producing beta cells from pancreatic tissue. They have long sought to improve the isolation and purification of beta cells, and space processing may be the answer. Consequently, a CFES experiment flown on the eighth shuttle flight, in August 1983, sought to determine the feasibility of producing highly purified beta cells in large quantities. Again, for commercial reasons, the results have not been released.

McDonnell Douglas also has either signed agreements or is negotiating with such organizations as the Summa Medical Corporation of Albuquerque, New Mexico; the

Lovelace Medical Foundation of Albuquerque; Scripps Institute of San Diego, California; and the Texas Medical Center of Houston—all aimed at the potential of developing space-based technologies and products.

The Lovelace Medical Center, for example, is studying space shuttle biological processing research that could result in new treatments for cancer and other diseases, such as malaria. This centers on the production of monoclonal antibodies in orbit and involves the fusing of harmful cells, such as cancer cells, with cells producing antibodies that fight diseases, such as lymphocyte cells.

When cancer cells are used, the result of the fusion process is hybrid cells that will multiply like cancer cells but produce antibodies that can kill or more easily identify harmful cancer cells in the body. The drug product from this research would be the antibodies produced by the hybrid cells. Research indicates more of the antibody material can be achieved from space-based processing than is possible in the earth's gravity. Malaria treatments could use the same principle applying the monoclonal process.

NASA has awarded annual grants of $450,000 to the University of Arizona in Tucson and the University City Science Center of Philadelphia, which involves nine universities and three medicine-related colleges, in hopes of stimulating biological research in space. This will focus on the areas of organic separations, bioprocessing, and pharmaceutical analysis. Additional support is being sought from industrial and educational sources.

"This is where the new products will come from," says James Rose, chief program engineer for McDonnell Douglas's electrophoresis program. "If you can help a researcher uncover the nature and source of a particular hormone or enzyme, then you can start a test program with another pharmaceutical product."

While it is still too early to predict how soon space processing of medical products will become a reality, or how large an industry it will spawn, at least one expert has already made some ambitious projections. John Yardley, president of McDonnell Douglas, forecasts that the production of new medicines in space will generate one billion dollars in sales by the early to mid-1990s—and this will be just for the first product. His company expects to be processing three different drugs in space by the mid-1990s and up to ten new drugs by the late 1990s. McDonnell Douglas also is giving serious consideration to building its own special factory spacecraft, which would be compatible with future permanent space stations.

The development of earth-orbiting pharmaceutical factories will cost billions of dollars, and this money will not be invested until it is determined that not only can new products be successfully made in space, but they also can be produced at a cost that will make it profitable to the manufacturers. The current experiments continue to show positive results, and it should be only a matter of time before other major companies across the United States and around the world join this grand endeavor.

In fact, the age of medicine processing in space likely will be upon us before the end of this century—and the beneficiaries will be the millions of sufferers of such dread diseases as diabetes and cancer.

CHAPTER TEN

HARNESSING NEW ENERGY SOURCES

It has taken the earth millions of years to form the oil, gas, and coal deposits from which the majority of our energy needs are drawn. If the earth's expanding population and accelerating standard of living continue to drain these precious resources at current or advanced levels, fossil fuels will eventually be depleted, possibly as early as sometime in the twenty-first century. And certainly, as the supplies dwindle, their costs will increase accordingly. There already have been warning signals. A shortage of oil sent gasoline and heating oil costs skyrocketing in the United States in the early 1970s, and millions of motorists waited long hours in line for gas at service stations nationwide.

For a long time, it was thought that nuclear power would offer a viable alternative to fossil fuels for the earth's needs. However, over the past twenty years, there has been a rising resistance among the general populace to the building and operation of nuclear plants. There is a widespread fear of radiation contamination should there be an accident

or leakage from such a plant. This was dramatically empha-
sized when an accident at a huge nuclear power facility,
at Three Mile Island in Pennsylvania, created fear across
the country. Since then, in the face of mounting criticism,
demonstrations, and multimillion-dollar lawsuits, many
nuclear plants have been closed or have curtailed operations,
and others, in various stages of planning or construction,
have been abandoned.

Solar power units, which convert the sun's virtually
boundless energy into useful forms on earth, have been installed in some homes, offices, and factories. But this has
been only on a relatively small scale, and in most instances
the harnessing of solar rays for this purpose is prohibitively
expensive. It likely will be decades before such technology
can be brought down to earth in terms of affordable costs to
the average consumer.

So the world's long-term energy problem remains un-
solved. Space offers some interesting and promising answers. Ultimately, scientists realize, the sun's enormous
power will have to be tamed and used. Solar energy is
nearly inexhaustible, pollution-free, and safe. "Importing
energy from the sun could become a future necessity," says
Richard Marsten, former director of communications programs for NASA, in 1983 in a special publication of Rockwell International, *This Is Why.*

He explains that a great deal of energy could be provided by "utilizing the solar power falling on earth, but the
systems to do this [currently] are limited by clouds, night,
real estate requirements, and transportation needs." However, Marsten says, "extraterrestrial systems which intercept
sunlight have virtually unlimited power potential."

The Solar Energy Panel, formed in the early 1970s by
the National Science Foundation and NASA, reported
early on that if sufficient money were spent on research,
solar energy could be supplying up to 35 percent of the
total building heating and cooling load, 30 percent of

American gas fuel requirements, 10 percent of liquid fuel needs, and 20 percent of the electrical power demand by the year 2020. The panel further stated that if large-scale solar energy use were realized, the United States could be saving three billion to four billion dollars annually on oil and gas by the year 2000.

Consequently, NASA issued a number of study contracts for assessing the feasibility of collecting solar power and channeling it through space for use on earth. The key to such a program, says Marsten, is the development of microwave technology for transmitting energy from extraterrestrial solar collection stations in orbit to the earth. Many power experts consider it only a matter of time until the technology can be developed.

One idea being considered by such large aerospace companies as Grumman and McDonnell Douglas calls for the establishment of large solar-energy collectors mounted on platforms in low orbit. Shuttles could service such platforms and bring the collected electrical power back to earth. Other companies, like Boeing and Raytheon, are looking into the practicality of building giant power-generating satellites that would directly beam solar power in space for immediate use on earth.

Various study programs envision solar collector panels as large as 22 square miles (57 sq km) placed in geosynchronous orbits 22,300 miles (35,903 km) out in space. The solar energy gathered by these panels would be converted to electrical power. A transmitter would then change the electrical power into a narrow microwave beam, which would be transmitted to earth where it would be received by antennas up to 5 miles (8 km) in diameter.

The microwave beam would be converted into direct current electrical energy and then into alternating current energy. One solar-cell satellite could provide 10,000 megawatts of electrical power—enough to supply a million households. Such a single satellite could produce twice the

An artist's rendering of one idea for a solar-powered laser system. The disk reflects light from the sun to a gas-filled tube, which emits a high-intensity light beam. This laser beam can be directed to various locations and transformed into conventional energy forms, such as electricity.

power generated by Grand Coulee, the nation's largest hydroelectric dam. Forty-five satellites could match the present total electrical generating power of the United States.

An entirely different concept now being given serious thought is the possibility of using lasers for transmitting solar power from orbit to earth. This idea has been gaining popularity as laser technology for development of space weapons has advanced in recent years.

Such a system would operate by using solar power on board a satellite to create a lasing gas, generating a high-energy laser beam. This beam would then be reflected by a mirror through space and the earth's atmosphere to an absorber on the ground. The resulting thermal energy could then be used to make steam or heat gas to drive turbine generators, as is done in conventional power plants.

A basic advantage of using lasers over microwaves is that their power can be transmitted over a much tighter beam. Consequently, the areas of the laser transmitters and receivers would be substantially smaller than the massive structures needed in the microwave designs. Since the laser transmitting device in orbit could be made so relatively small, it would be possible to construct all the laser power-generating equipment in a lower, sun-synchronous earth orbit near the North and South poles so that it would remain in full sunlight all the time.

The smaller equipment also would cut costs of launching and servicing the system. Further, the small size of the receiving station on the earth would enable its location close to centers of most power demand, such as large cities. It is even conceivable that the laser receiving station could be tied into existing utility switchyards, which would greatly simplify ground distribution and transmission. Utility power plants might even be able to replace their old steam-generating units with laser-heated boilers and superheaters.

The major drawback at this time to employing a laser

solar power system is that the technology for developing it is not nearly as far along as is the microwave system. It will take years, possibly decades, before such a design can move from the drawing board to hardware practicality. Still, its tremendous long-range potential deserves continued serious research and study.

Perhaps the ultimate answer to the world's energy problems is also one of the simplest, at least on paper: the use of visible light for energy transmission. If a way can be found to eliminate the "inconvenience" of clouds, bad weather, and nightfall, then the earth could bask in an electric-power-generating system using only sunlight.

How would such a continuous solar power system work? Through the use of giant mirrors to reflect sunlight to ground-based solar power plants. The idea is not new. It was first considered by space pioneer Hermann Oberth in 1929. Another original space thinker, Krafft Ehricke, advanced the concept a generation later by proposing mirrors to illuminate the earth. By deploying a complex of mirrors nearly a square mile in diameter in geosynchronous orbit, Ehricke told the author, "You will have a means of illuminating thirty-six thousand square miles (93,000 sq km) of earth surface without disturbing ecological effects. This can be done by solar reflection, involving no power consumption and therefore no pollution on earth.

"The area would be illuminated to about ten times the full moon's brightness on a clear night, and several times the full moon's brightness when in the presence of a cloud cover. Can you imagine the effects of such a phenomenon? Benefits range from greater public safety in urban areas to agricultural advantages in being able to work in the cool of night in tropical regions."

For power generation, a large number of circular flat mirrors could be placed in various orbits, each directing sunlight to the collectors of several ground-based solar electric power plants, in turn, as the structure passes over them. The orbiting mirrors would increase the power-generating capability of each plant during the day, when the sun is shining, and also keep it operating at night.

While Ehricke envisioned mirrors in orbit 22,300 miles (35,903 km) above the earth, later design proposals call for placement in much lower orbits. One study suggests using sixty thousand mirrors, each just over half a mile in diameter and weighing about three tons, in an orbit roughly 3,000 miles (4,830 km) above the equator. From here, the reflected beams of sunlight could illuminate five large solar power plants on the ground, each capable of generating an average power of 130,000 megawatts from natural plus mirror-augmented sunlight. The total electric power produced by just these five plants would be equal to twice the entire current U.S. electric power consumption. Again, however, while this concept appears feasible, it awaits further technological developments.

Also, the mirror system, like the microwave and laser designs, will need an initial commitment by the U.S. government. The development of any of these programs is far too expensive and time-consuming to be undertaken by private industry. The problem, for at least the past dozen years, has been more political and bureaucratic than anything else. Although NASA originally was supportive of developing a solar energy system, it was phased out of the picture in 1974 with the passage of the Solar Energy Act. This transferred the responsibility to the U.S. Energy Research and Development Administration, which later became the Department of Energy.

This agency, following a three-year, $15-million evaluation study in the late 1970s, effectively shelved the program, considering it too vague and expensive to commit the funds and motivation needed to get it off the launching pad. However, with President Reagan's later backing of the goal of building a space station, the early renewal of a solar energy project appears more likely.

There is no question that it will come in time. The sun's power will become a necessity, not a dream, within the next half century. And with it will come a vast new industry which will harness the sun's rays to provide earth's power needs of the future.

CHAPTER ELEVEN

AN ENTREPRENEURIAL DREAM

Many of the benefits to mankind that will come from the future exploitation of space are, today, unknown. It is easily perceived that applications arising from current research activities will continue to expand. No one can yet comprehend the full dimensions of the possibilities that commercialization of space can generate for the service of humanity.

In fact, some of the most beneficial and most profound results may accrue in areas where the benefits are indirect. These could include international relations, management techniques for complex businesses, and industrial technology. Certainly, one of the most significant results will be in the advance of knowledge, the understanding of the evolution of the universe and of the origins of life.

Meanwhile, more tangible are some new interesting space business ventures now in the works.

One of the most popular programs NASA has introduced to date, and one that strongly encourages new ideas, products, and techniques leading toward commercialization of space, is called the Getaway Special. It is a program that offers companies, even individuals, a chance to test their experiment by flying it into orbit in small "leftover" spaces on the shuttle at reasonable costs of three thousand to ten thousand dollars.

NASA introduced the Getaway Specials on the fourth shuttle flight, in November 1982, with the purpose of "seeking to stimulate broader interest in space research by the large segment of the scientific and industrial community not engaged in development of primary payloads." Each package, which is restricted to from 2.5 to 5 cubic feet (.07–.14 cu m) in volume, and from 60 to 200 pounds (27–91 kg) in weight, must be of a scientific or industrial research nature.

The program has proven so popular that there is a long waiting list of hundreds of prospective users, and several small companies have gone into the business of supplying support, equipment, and systems to the researchers.

"This provides a means for developing basic space expertise and building blocks for future programs," says Jim Barrowman, NASA's manager of the Getaway Specials. "These flights are giving students and companies, large and small, a chance to learn about space research. I think many of them are just realizing that they may have a potentially viable commercial application."

Some of the payloads that have flown to date have included: seed germination and sprouting experiments, electrophoresis-related experiments, tests of microorganism development, electroplating in zero gravity, metal solidification studies, fluid dynamics experiments, and various metal-joining tests.

In the future, if Getaway Special experiments prove promising, customers may enlarge their packages up to 1,000 pounds (455 kg) in a new program called Hitchhiker. Or they may buy space in regular shuttle payload areas. This is where the real market for materials processing and commercialization will develop, says John Cassanto, president of Instrumentation Technology Associates, one of the companies that helps clients package their experiments for shuttle flights.

One industry that is expected to grow by leaps and bounds in the immediate years ahead is space insurance. The launching of rockets and sophisticated, heavily instrumented spacecraft into orbit is an enormously expensive venture costing tens of millions of dollars for each flight. And while the reliability of boosters and of satellite systems has improved tremendously since the early days, rockets occasionally still blow up, and satellites still malfunction.

Many companies, especially the young, entrepreneurial types, could not survive such a catastrophic event without insurance. When the space shuttle first began its test flights, in the early 1980s, the space insurance business seemed ready to soar itself. James Barrett, chairman of the first company organized exclusively to provide space insurance, enthusiastically predicted in 1981, "We expect up to two billion dollars in premiums in the next decade."

But when three satellites failed during the first half of 1984, causing astronomical claims, the fledgling space insurance business had to pull in its horns, and rethink whether or not this would be a good industry to be in. This has caused insurance companies to either limit coverage or raise the cost of coverage to exorbitant levels.

Obviously, as the reliability of the shuttle and of proven expendable launch vehicle systems improve with experience, this will enable insurers to reduce costs and expand coverage. Meanwhile, Congress is looking into the possibility of supplementing space insurance. Whatever happens, however, space insurance is a business that will be essential as private industry takes over more and more of the risks of doing business in space.

Two other fledgling industries that show tremendous potential for application in space are transportation and tourism. Today, it takes six or seven hours to fly from the United States to Europe. Some experts believe rocket-powered craft, using technology and concepts developed for the space shuttle, will be able to whisk passengers to sites halfway around the world in forty-five minutes or less.

Such vehicles would be launched vertically in suborbital trajectories aimed at a precise destination. They would reenter the atmosphere and glide unpowered to an altitude where conventional jet engines would be started to control the descent and landing on conventional runways.

The only prohibiting factor for such accelerated flights is cost. But since it takes much less energy to put an object in earth orbit than it does to fly the same object across the United States, there is no reason why, in time, the cost of rocket-powered flight should not become competitive with conventional means of travel.

Once space has been opened up to routine, tourist-type travel—and it will be, possibly before the end of the century—a whole new industry will evolve. The first flights may be too expensive for the ordinary citizen, but costs will come down once the trail has been blazed.

Paul Siegler, president of Earth/Space, a California consulting firm contracted to NASA to study the impact of space industrialization over the next thirty years, says initial flights would cost over fifty thousand dollars, but once a space "hotel" has been established, round trips to earth orbit might be made for five thousand dollars or less. Interest in such travel already is keen. Pan American Airways, for example, has booked more than ninety thousand reservations for flights to the moon. Says Siegler, "I see a hundred-room hotel up there [in space] in about the year 2000, when the tourist traffic really starts to move."

Certainly one of the most unusual commercial ventures in space is being offered by an organization called the Celestis Group, in Melbourne, Florida, only a few miles from the launching pads of NASA's Kennedy Space Center. Celestis includes several engineers and morticians, headed by John Cherry, a funeral director.

For a fee of $3,900, this group will rocket the cremated remains of loved ones into an orbit 1,900 miles (3,059 km) above the earth. The human ashes will be encapsulated and identified by name, Social Security number, and religious symbol. Cherry says one rocket nose cone could contain as many as thirteen thousand capsules, each ⅜ inch (.95 cm) by 1¼ inch (3.18 cm) in size.

Other mortician groups also are interested in space burials. One is a company in Tyler, Texas, known as Starbound. Its president, Rusty Miller, foresees a large market once the concept is accepted. In an interview with the *New York Times* in January 1985, he said, "People like to have their ashes spread over the ocean, and there is no bigger ocean than the cosmic ocean."

The ever-growing promise of private industry's increasing role in space encouraged the launching of yet another new venture in the spring of 1985—the start of a new magazine called *Commercial Space*. It is published by McGraw-Hill, in New York City, and its editors report enthusiastic reception. Early issues of the publication have been chock-full of advertising touting the capabilities of many young, space-oriented companies.

Further out into the future, perhaps early in the twenty-first century, mining in space will blossom into a new industry that could grow to gigantic proportions, supplying the earth for hundreds of years with precious minerals and other resources that are becoming scarcer every day on this planet.

"Take the moon," says space visionary Dr. Krafft Ehricke. "Here, we have a raw material source, a huge motherlode, if you will, orbiting in the sky. We could move industry to the moon and space-truck clean materials back to earth. It doesn't matter if mankind pollutes the moon a little, or exploits its resources. The business of earth is life. The fifty-two million square miles (2.964 billion sq km) of land on earth are the most precious real estate in the

Above: *an artist's concept of lunar mining
operations for the production of liquid oxygen.
Ilmenite, a fairly common, oxygen-rich component
of lunar soil, is the material being mined. At center,
a robot front-end loader scoops out lunar soil.*
Facing page: *an illustration of a space solar power
system surrounded by the activity of asteroid retrieval.
Creation of a new economy in space is the
objective of retrieving an asteroid to high Earth-orbit.
Asteroids contain many of the major elements that
provide the basis for industry and life on earth.*

solar system. Let these other dead worlds be a place for industry.

"Among our sister worlds that are reasonably accessible to us—the moon, Mars, Mercury, the asteroids—are treasure houses of minerals and all the other elements that human minds and tools will need to supply mankind," Dr. Ehricke says.

Even now, engineers are working on designs for powerful electromagnetic engines that could dislodge asteroids from their solar orbits and push them into near-earth orbits where they could be mined whenever new mineral supplies were needed on the earth.

CHAPTER TWELVE

PRO AND CON

The practicality of celestial mining is, of course, still a long way off in the future—perhaps several decades. And this brings up a point that should be aired in any detailed discussion of the commercialization of space. That is, simply, no one really knows exactly how long it will take before space can be harnessed on a broad scale for the manufacture of products and services on a profitable basis.

Some optimistic concerns have said they believe certain commercial products can be produced in orbit to make the venture worthwhile for investors by as early as the late 1980s. Others believe it will be at least the 1990s, or even the early twenty-first century, before this happens.

And there are critics and skeptics who contend it will be much longer, perhaps a half century or more, if ever, before manufacturing in space becomes a routine business.

These critics make a good argument. Basically, they say, the start-up costs, even with government subsidy and support, are still far too high to reap any near-term financial returns. And this has been a sticking point that new space companies are finding hard to overcome in trying to attract private investors.

These companies have grown rapidly, from only a handful in 1980 to several dozen today, but they are finding the going tough because of the perceived risks, the large amounts of money required, and the relatively long delay in potential return on investment.

Jerome Simonoff, vice-president of Citicorp Industrial Credit, agrees with many of his colleagues in saying the underlying issue involved in space system financing is its high cost, often ranging in the tens of millions of dollars. That is why many companies entering this new arena of commerce are doing so in joint efforts with others—to share the costs.

Simonoff says he would like to see as much government-supplied service as possible, and believes NASA should lower business entry costs as an incentive. "When start-up costs come down, you will have more investment," he notes.

This aside, critics also point to the high risk associated with an industry still in its infancy. Such risks are most dramatically manifested in the failure of launch vehicles and complex, sophisticated satellites. This has been especially true in the field of communications satellites.

The malfunction of two Leasat spacecraft, for example, in 1985 caused a loss of $170 million. Coupled with other misfirings in space, more than $350 million was lost on communications satellites during an eighteen-month period from 1984 through mid-1985.

While a considerable portion of this was covered by insurance, it caused a complete shake-up of insurance coverage of space flights. As a direct result of the Leasat failures, International Technology Underwriters (Intec) announced it was dropping out of the space launch insurance market, and would underwrite satellite insurance coverage in the future only after spacecraft have been delivered to their proper orbits.

"Let the satellite manufacturer bear the risk of successful performance of his satellite," said James W. Barrett, Intec president. "Perhaps he will be motivated to achieve higher levels of design control and quality assurance. In no future underwriting will Intec insure the performance of a communications satellite prior to its successful positioning and operation in orbit and delivery to the owner."

The failure of a French Ariane rocket to boost its high-priced satellite cargo into orbit, also in mid-1985, further added to the fears of users.

In May 1986, another Ariane was destroyed shortly after launch from French Guiana when its third stage failed to ignite while enroute to orbit. This caused European officials to ground further Ariane flights until a thorough investigation of the rocket's problems could be conducted and analyzed.

This disaster was compounded when a U.S. Delta rocket, laden with a weather satellite, blew up seventy-one seconds after being launched from the Kennedy Space Center, also in May 1986. A month earlier, a $65 million Air Force Titan rocket, carrying a secret spy satellite, exploded shortly after takeoff at the Vandenberg launch site in California.

All of these catastrophies, on top of the space shuttle Challenger tragedy in January 1986 (see author's note, page 112), sent the space program—in the United States and worldwide—into shock. Satellite flight schedules were canceled or postponed for several months. In fact, the whole question of insurance of space-related projects is undergoing a complete reevaluation. When such insurance is available, it is extremely expensive. This could well prove to be another area where the federal government will have to get involved more extensively until the reliability of launch vehicles and spacecraft improves.

There are other factors, too, that make critics question just how near the day of practical space commercialization is. The pullout of the Ortho subsidiary of Johnson and

Johnson after years of space research in partnership with McDonnell Douglas is one prime example of the many as yet unresolved problems of doing business in space.

But, proponents counter, every major new industry or new technology went through similar periods. In the early days of aviation, they say, there were many crashes, disasters, and setbacks at a time when no one could envision the enormous benefits that are reaped today from the development and maturity of the airline industry.

Virtually no one questions the fact that the problems, in time, will be solved, and the eventual rewards will prove beneficial to all on earth—to both the makers and the users of space-related products and services.

Author's Note:

On January 28, 1986, the space shuttle *Challenger* was destroyed when a giant rocket booster tank exploded during flight, a little more than a minute after liftoff from the Kennedy Space Center in Florida. The entire crew of seven, including New Hampshire school teacher Christa McAuliffe, was killed.

An investigation was launched soon after to find the cause of the spectacular accident. Future shuttle flights were postponed indefinitely, and, in a sense, the whole U.S. space program was put on "temporary hold."

President Ronald Reagan put the *Challenger* disaster in perspective as well as anyone when he said, speaking of the astronauts, "They had a hunger to explore the universe and discover its truths. . . . They served all of us." Then, talking specifically to the nation's students, he said, "I know it's hard to understand that sometimes painful things like this happen. It's all part of the process of exploration and discovery, it's all part of taking a chance and expanding man's horizons."

After several months of exhaustive investigations, it was determined that faulty seals in the shuttle's solid rocket booster engines had malfunctioned, leading to the explosion.

NASA was given the charge to completely redesign these engines—a task estimated to take a year or longer.

Meanwhile, in April 1986, the Air Force awarded contracts worth between $300 million and $400 million to industries for the development of a new aerospace plane. This is to be equipped with scramjet engines that burn their fuel in an airstream that moves at supersonic speeds. The plane is expected to be capable of taking off from a runway and quickly accelerating to speeds twelve to twenty-five times the speed of sound.

With the aid of a built-in rocket, the plane could climb above the atmosphere and into a low orbit of earth. Planners for both the military and NASA see the aerospace plane as becoming a more versatile, efficient, and lower cost means of delivering people and payloads to space than conventional rockets or the shuttle.

Still another turn in the fast-evolving U.S. space policy took place in August 1986. The Reagan administration told NASA that it should phase out the business of launching commercial satellites altogether. President Reagan said this job "can be done faster and cheaper by the private sector." This came closely on the heels of Reagan's approval of a new orbiter vehicle to be built to replace the destroyed *Challenger*.

The decision to get NASA out of the commercial satellite launch business was a controversial one, because launching such vehicles was one of the key points in justifying the expensive shuttle program in the first place. Secondly, it left a huge backlog of unlaunched satellites.

Most U.S. aerospace companies said it would take them at least two to three years to build a launch vehicle capability. That left satellite owners with few options to get their current spacecraft into orbit. One would be to go with foreign launch operations, such as France's Ariane rocket. But the Ariane also was having its problems, and already was overbooked for flights.

While some experts were critical of the administration's

decision, others felt it would free the shuttle to fly mostly military missions and to become a "flying repair van" increasingly devoted to those projects that require humans in space, such as fixing failed satellites and performing unusually complicated launchings or experiments. It would also continue to have a key role in the development of the U.S. space station in years to come.

"In some ways that may be better for the nation and more realistic for us," said Philip Culbertson, NASA's general manager.

But nearly everyone agreed that the shuttle would continue to be a major factor in the coming day of orbiting factories and the commercialization of space.

CHAPTER THIRTEEN

THE SPACE STATION AND BEYOND

"Our goal is to build on America's pioneer spirit and develop our next frontier," President Ronald Reagan said in his State of the Union speech, January 25, 1984. "A sparkling economy spurs initiative, sunrise industries, and makes older ones competitive.

"Nowhere is this more true than our next frontier: space. Nowhere do we so effectively demonstrate our technological leadership. . . . Our progress in space—taking giant steps for all mankind—is a tribute to American teamwork and excellence. . . .

"America has always been greatest when we dare to be great . . . we can follow our dreams to distant stars, living and working in space for peaceful, economic, and scientific gain. . . .

"Tonight, I am directing NASA to develop a permanently manned space station, and to do it within a decade."

Three days later, in a national radio address, the president added: "A space station will not be an end in itself, but a doorway to even greater progress in the future. In this case, a space station will open up new opportunities for expanding human commerce and learning."

The president called for a partnership of government and industry in the development and utilization of the space station. He also invited America's friends and allies to participate in the program.

The idea for such a working outpost in space is not new. It has been envisioned for more than forty years by such farsighted experts as the great German rocket scientist Dr. Wernher von Braun. But it was not until the space shuttle proved itself as a reliable space transportation system in the 1980s, that the station could be considered a realistic, relatively short-term goal.

Potential users include the science and applications communities, national security interests, the aerospace industry, a broad spectrum of commercial interests, high technology industries, and international technology developers.

The U.S. space station is intended to serve multiple functions. It will enable commercial production—in quantity—of critical materials not available on the earth, where gravity exerts adverse influences on manufacturing processes. It also will serve as a scientific laboratory for research in such fields as astrophysics, solar system exploration, earth science, and life sciences. It will be used as a testing ground for developing technology in such areas as communications and nonspace applications, and as a base for further research in materials processing.

The station will be a permanent facility for tending, servicing, and repairing satellites and unmanned platforms. Additionally, it will permit in-orbit assembly of large structures such as antennas, telescopes, and experiment modules. And for the longer term, it will offer a staging area for twenty-first-century missions, such as a permanent lunar base, manned survey flights to the asteroids, or manned missions to other planets.

*NASA is developing a design for a permanently-manned
space station to be in operation by the mid-1990s.
The station will provide a work platform for
conducting experiments related to space physics,
astronomy, life sciences, and material sciences.
It also will provide areas for commercial endeavors.*

NASA is studying a number of different station concepts. Current thinking calls for two unmanned platforms plus the main base. One of them, carrying instruments and experiments for scientific and product research, will operate in the same orbit as the main base, but some distance removed from it to avoid disturbance or contamination from main-station activities; the second platform will operate in a different orbit. The platform can be visited by astronauts equipped with maneuvering units for routine inspection and maintenance; for payload recovery and refurbishment, the platform can be retrieved by an orbital maneuvering vehicle and brought to the main base.

The central station will have a large solar power system generating 75 kilowatts and each of the platforms will have solar arrays providing 25 to 35 kilowatts. The manned base will have four or more pressurized modules wherein a crew of six to eight will live and work, plus the docking hub for the shuttle orbiter and a utilities system supplying electrical power, thermal control, attitude control, and data processing facilities. The space shuttle will be the station's link to the earth, resupplying it and rotating crews at intervals of three to six months.

Overall, the elements that are likely to make up the first station will include an energy module, assembly and berthing module, habitat modules, logistics module, space processing laboratory module, payload service assembly, propellant module, and research and development module.

These modules probably will be built on earth and transported to orbit by the shuttle. There, they will be connected to each other and built up in sequence to develop greater flexibility and potential usage. Thus, the station may be constructed gradually over a period of months or longer.

The modules in which astronauts, scientists, and business representatives will live will provide a pressurized "shirt sleeve" environment. That is, the living area will have the same constituents and pressure as air at sea level. Such an artificial gravity, in the weightlessness of space, can be created by swinging the station like a pendulum counterbalanced by a spent rocket booster stage, which might be connected by long cables. Of course, there also will be areas of zero gravity in which experiments can be conducted in the pure vacuum of space. There will be comfortable quarters for working, eating, sleeping, and general recreation and relaxation.

There will be subsystems, such as environmental control, to maintain a pure, breathable atmosphere, and water management, to reclaim waste water for reuse. Crew members can be rotated on a regular basis, but probably would stay in space three to six months or even longer.

The station should have an operational life in orbit of at least ten years. The modular structures will allow additions at any time. The core station could weigh up to 100,000 pounds (453,602 kg). To keep morale high and to stimulate creative and effective work, considerable care will be taken in decorating and stocking the living facilities. Food preparation and service will be as close as possible to that on earth; fresh-frozen meats and vegetables will be available.

Because the cost of constructing, assembling, and operating such a station will be tremendously high, developmental costs will be assumed by the federal government, through NASA. However, in time, responsibility for the facility—its management and maintenance—will be turned over to private enterprise.

In time, other stations will follow, enabling large-scale manufacturing operations and materials processing in space that are difficult or impossible to accomplish on earth. Once this capability has been achieved, whole new orders of precision, flawless products and pure drugs, vaccines and pharmaceuticals, will be produced on a routine basis and flown back to the earth for use. This will foster the era of true space factories. The potential for future, as yet unknown, applications of the space sation will be limited only by people's imagination.

Consider some possibilities. The enormous benefits derived from operational weather satellites, for example, are well known. But think what it would be like to add the forecasting potential of professional meteorologists using advanced instruments and making direct observations of weather phenomena from a space station. Imagine the contributions to protecting the earth's resources or increasing productivity a geologist could make, or an agricultural expert, a forester, a hydrologist, an oceanographer—they could interpret and analyze raw information obtained in flight, selecting what to transmit to earth.

The station will be a fixed space research facility for conducting scientific investigations to extend our knowledge of the nature of the universe. The station will offer life scientists the opportunity to study life processes under conditions impossible to duplicate on earth. Significant advances will result from long-term study in space of plants and animals, including humans, by doctors, biologists, botanists, and others.

With an orbiting station as the centerpiece, various structures can be assembled in its immediate vicinity, such as hugh antennas, mirrors, and reflectors—for energy collection and transmission, for communications, or for a variety of other applications.

And the station will be the first building block in the inevitable establishment of permanent space bases.

Sometime in the twenty-first century will come orbital colonies and communities—whole cities in space. This will create a space-based construction boom, and beyond it all the attendant service and manufacturing facilities to sustain life high above the earth.

"The first three-dimensional civilization will soon be born," says Dr. Ehricke, "creating a civilization in which earth becomes the center of a vast and growing sphere of human activity encompassing surrounding space and other worlds. Space orbits are the new lands of our time and in the decades and centuries to come. Space stations will be the historical, but comparatively modest, first step on a journey that knows no end."

With the opening up of the commercialization of space, that journey has begun.

INDEX

A B O U T   T H E
AUTHOR

L. B. Taylor, Jr., is the author of many books for young adults on topics of national concern, including *Driving High: The Hazards of Driving, Drinking and Drugs; The Nuclear Arms Race*; and *Space: Battleground of the Future*. Most recently he co-authored *Chemical and Biological Warfare*, with C. L. Taylor.

A former employee of the National Aeronautics and Space Administration (NASA), Mr. Taylor now lives and works in Williamsburg, Virginia.